Made For More

Finding Hope In The Midst Of Darkness

Winter Hall

WESTBOW
PRESS®
A DIVISION OF THOMAS NELSON
& ZONDERVAN

WestBow Press books may be ordered through booksellers or by contacting:

WestBow Press
A Division of Thomas Nelson & Zondervan
1663 Liberty Drive
Bloomington, IN 47403
www.westbowpress.com
844-714-3454

ISBN: 978-1-6642-7535-5 (sc)
ISBN: 978-1-6642-7536-2 (hc)
ISBN: 978-1-6642-7534-8 (e)

Library of Congress Control Number: 2022915134

Print information available on the last page.

WestBow Press rev. date: 8/23/2022

Contents

In loving memory of my dad.

Preface

My hope and prayer is that these stories of hope will inspire you to seek a deeper relationship with God and realize that even though the darkness seems too much to bear, you are stronger and braver than you know. You are loved by someone who died for you. You are not alone. Your story isn't over. You are worthy. You were created with purpose. You are beautiful.

The following stories recount personal struggles, conversations, thoughts, and prayers I feel God has put on my heart to share. I've had a recurring message ever since a specific moment in 2016 that I'll share with you in the following pages. God has continued to say, "Just share your story." Through reliving these struggles and experiences, I've learned some things that can help others.

I would love for every word in this book to sink into the depths of your soul and light a fire there; however, if you get nothing else, my deepest prayer is that you, my friend, know you are not alone. No matter how alone you feel, you aren't. God created you. He loved you enough to send his Son to die for you.

Your life experiences aren't my life experiences. Just because my experiences had certain outcomes, it doesn't mean yours will turn out the same way. I hope this inspires you to seek God for yourself. Seek him in the good times and the bad. Remember the times you didn't think you could make it and he brought you through. Take time to see the beauty and blessings in the midst of your struggles.

I'm not going to tell you that if you do this or that your life will be perfect or that bad things won't happen; that's not the case at all. Often when you decide you want to live a purposeful life for God, you will face trials. Living for God isn't easy, but it's definitely worth it. The biggest life lesson I've learned is that it's not about me—my hurt, my pain, my joy, or my wants. It's about God. Friend, I know how incredibly frustrating this fact can be. Just because I've learned this truth doesn't mean that struggles are any easier, but I want to show how this moment can be used to help someone else while glorifying God.

I pray you will take some time to really reflect after reading each day. This devotional is meant to be used to dig deeper into, not only yourself, but your relationship with God as well.

My hope and prayer is that each time you read from this book, you can find something in the writings to connect with and find comfort in.

Friend, I want you to know I'm praying for you. I'm rooting for you. You've got this! Most importantly, *keep fighting*! Always remember you are loved and never alone.

Introduction

When I lost my dad I searched for books that talked about grief—especially ones in which a little girl lost her dad. I combed through bookstores, googled it, and even checked Amazon, but I couldn't find anything I really liked. I was so full of all these feelings and questions, and I just wanted something to read and connect with. A fleeting thought hit me—*I should write something myself.* I'd often open up my laptop and start the first sentence, but I never got past the first page. A few times I even made *just getting started* my New Year's resolution. Over the last sixteen years the thought of writing the book has often come to mind, but I just kept dragging my feet. Now I have to wonder whether there was a reason for the book I intended to write never getting past more than a couple sentences.

There have been so many moments when I have desperately wanted to read something I connected with. There have been so many times when I've thought, *I can't take this anymore. I can't keep going.* Maybe there are others out there who could be helped by my stories. I often keep silent when I am struggling and rarely ever let anyone in on what's truly going on. There are so many moments in my life I can write about that lead to this moment. This past year I had a lot of alone time with my thoughts and felt compelled to write these down in the notes of my phone. I wrote about these moments in this book, but it was really just recently asking God why—again. Why has everything up until this moment in my life happened if nothing good was going to come of it? What was the point in going through all of these things?

When I think back over my life, I have always been a nobody. I was never meant to be anything or make a difference—never meant to make a change. Yet here I sit. Why? I'm not trying to sound conceited. My heart is full of passion to help others, but I feel unqualified—to be an inspiration to others. If my suffering can help someone else, then it's OK. In that moment I realized maybe everything I'd experienced had happened so I could write about it.

I've often read plans in my Bible app, but I've never fully loved any of them. I was always wishing there was something I could better connect to. I've tried reading some inspirational books, and I've enjoyed some, while finding others too "churchy." I want to relate to the writer. I want to feel what the writer feels. I want to connect to them and feel like they've been where I am. I want them to feel real. So often we've seen preachers, teachers, and Christian artists and authors as unrelatable—like they're superhuman. Like they don't make mistakes and sin!

I don't want to write like someone else. I want to write from my heart. I want to be real. This book contains real stories from my life—real pain, *real joy*. These are real thoughts, feelings, and prayers that I've actually thought, felt, and prayed. I am not some superhuman. I am not someone to look up to. I'm just a nobody girl from a small town struggling to live the life God created me for. I've spent my entire life hiding in the crowds, too scared to eat in front of people, and never wanting to talk because I felt judged for my childlike Southern drawl. I was so afraid of failure I even hid the idea of writing this book from my husband, because I doubt myself so much.

I was born and raised in Millen, Georgia, and for the first three years of my life I lived in a single-wide trailer. Then we moved in with my mom's mom for a year while my dad was building my parents' dream home. In 1984, when I was three, we moved into the house. I stayed there until I was twenty-four and married my high school sweetheart. In 2005 I graduated from Georgia Southern University with a bachelor's degree in business administration. On June 25, 2005, my dad walked me down the aisle, holding me up while my legs shook with nervous energy. I could see the twinkle in his eyes, and neither spoke of what we knew this moment meant. In a few short hours I would be leaving this place I'd called home and the people I loved to move with my husband to Dallas, Texas. This move would only be the beginning of a long journey of discovering who I really am and where God will take me.

Before I can really get started on how and why this book came to be, I have to go back in time a little to share the most instrumental moments in my life along the way. Here's where it all started.

I'd said the sinner's prayer a few times over the course of my teenage years, but I honestly didn't grasp the full impact of it—nor did I truly change when I uttered the words. In July of 1998, I was invited to and attended a summer church camp. One afternoon the camp attendees were meeting on the dock of the camp's lake, when a woman who'd been brought in from the church came to speak to us. I remember her praying and speaking to my heart, and for the first time, when I said the prayer all the walls I'd built up came crashing down. In that moment, I knew God had rescued me. God reached down into the depths of despair and pulled me out of the darkness I had been hiding in for a long time. I can't describe the feeling, but I came away from that camp a different person. I was finally free. I released the pain and hurt I'd carried for so long. In that moment I felt a love I'd never felt before. I started attending church regularly. I was even part of a vacation Bible school skit there. That is where my best friend started to become my best friend. We'd gone to school together since he'd moved to my hometown in first grade; however, we'd spent most of our lives not really noticing—and at times not even liking—each other.

Sometimes we don't recognize our journeys while we're on them, but later we can look back and see the pieces of God's plans falling into place. Had I not gone to that camp, God may not have saved me in that moment. Had God not saved me, I may not have ended up attending that church frequently. Had I not attended that church on Sundays or been a part of that VBS, I may not have become best friends with my now husband. Going through life is hard. We may not always see God moving and working and may not even understand why things happen as they do, but it's OK, friend; we don't have too. God is in control if we will allow Him to be.

On that dock in 1998 at the church camp, I heard and felt these words: "If you will take up your cross daily and follow Me ..." Every moment since has been about these words. I didn't leave that camp "saved" to just go through life. I left that camp with a desire, not only to please God, but to do whatever He has called me to do and be who He called me to be. I will say what God has called me to say, even when it's hard—when I'm tired, when I don't feel qualified, when I feel unworthy, when I feel unloved, when I feel like a nobody. I'll heed His calling even when I feel like a failure, when the tears are streaming down my face, and when I feel like my world is falling apart. Even when my marriage is on the brink of destruction, when I have no faith or hope, when I have given everything I can give and have nothing left, I will do what God commands. At the end of this journey, I want to know I kept going even when I thought I couldn't. I didn't give up. I learned, and I grew. If my story, my struggles, my pain, and my determination can help one person, it's all worth it, which leads me to the greatest moment that has shaped the rest of my life thus far and the most influential moment that led to the writing of this devotional.

Most of us have a day in our lives that we'll never forget. For some this day was full of joy and wonder. For others this day was full of sorrow and hurt. What was this day for you? I can clearly remember just about every moment of, not only this day, but the few days leading up to it. It was a Friday, and we'd made the long trek home like usual. We picked up a pizza from Pizza Hut for dinner. (It was a shock that our small town actually had one at that time.) My dad wanted to get out of bed, and although my brother and husband tried to help, they unintentionally hurt him instead. He didn't make it out of the bed that night, so we sat with him in my old room. It was November, so I'm sure we were watching a football game. Knowing him, it was the Georgia game.

On Sunday I woke up with this feeling that I just didn't want to go back to Chattanooga, where we were living at the time. Something inside just kept saying, *Stay*. But reluctantly, at 3:00 p.m., we headed home so we could go to work the next week. The whole way home, I was silent. My gut kept telling me it wasn't long. Over and over in my head, I just kept thinking, *Turn around, turn around; just go back*. As we got off 75 onto East Brainerd Road, I started to cry—as I always did at this point of every trip home from my Dad's—but this time was different. My husband looked at me and asked what was wrong. I kept looking out the window as tears rolled down my cheeks, and I barely mustered out the words, "We will be lucky if he makes it to Wednesday."

I got home, and all I could think was, *He's dying, and I'm not there*. I didn't get any sleep that night, and when I got to work on Monday morning, my brother called me. He said they'd called the nurse, and Dad wasn't doing well. They weren't sure how much longer he was going to make it. I immediately called my husband and set off to pack my bags. I stopped by his work before heading out for the five-hour drive back home. I cried the whole way there. I took a deep breath as I opened the door. When I walked into the house I grew up in, it was full of silent people. My dad's mom was in the room with him when I got there. To be honest, I knew when I walked into the house that I needed God to overtake my mind, my body, and my soul.

There is no doubt that I am a Daddy's girl. My father gave me everything I wanted. He rarely if ever told me no. While my friends were off having fun at parties or at other girls' houses, I was at home playing rummy with my dad. He'd get off from work and just come sit in my room and watch TV with me. We didn't have to speak much to know he was my daddy and I was his little girl. Even at twenty-five, I was still his little girl. I avoided going into the room as long as I could, because I knew what I had to do. I knew what I had to say. To be honest, I wasn't really sure I actually could say it. God and I had a lot of talks about what would happen if I lost my dad. I knew God could heal him, but I also knew that wasn't going to be God's plan. So I finally got the courage after my mom told me to go see him in the room. I knew that once I was beside his bed, I wouldn't want to leave him. People came and visited, but I remained. At one point my mom came to stay beside him, and at around 10:00 p.m., my brother and I went to my aunt's house next door to get old Christmas movies we'd made growing up.

It was around 11:00 when my brother said he was going to bed. He headed off to his room. My mom and brother were tired; they hadn't gotten much sleep after I'd left the night before. My dad had to be given pain medicine every four hours by a dropper in the mouth. I told them to go to bed; I'd stay up with him. I looked at my brother and said, "Do you?"

He said, "No."

I said, "OK."

We both knew what I was talking about—he didn't want to be around when my dad took his last breath.

Everyone had gone to bed. It was about 4:00 in the morning

when I looked down at my dad and said, "It's OK. I'm OK. I will be OK. I have an amazing husband who loves me and will take care of me. Mom will be OK. Grandma will be OK. We will be OK. You're tired. It's OK; go be with your dad. It's OK to let go." He couldn't speak, but he opened his eyes that were full of tears and made a sound. I asked if he wanted mom, and he nodded his head. So I went to wake Mom up. We sat by his bed. I laid my head down for a moment because I had been up at this point for well over twenty-four hours, and then I heard my mom say, "Jimmie." I quickly raised my head to see my mom shaking my dad. He wasn't breathing. My mom was saying "Jimmie," and I was saying, "Daddy." It took a second, but he jumped and opened his eyes, looked at us, closed his eyes, and took his last breath at 5:34 a.m., Tuesday, November 7, 2006. Had I not met Jesus on that hot summer July day, I think the story that comes from this soul-wrenching pain would be a lot different.

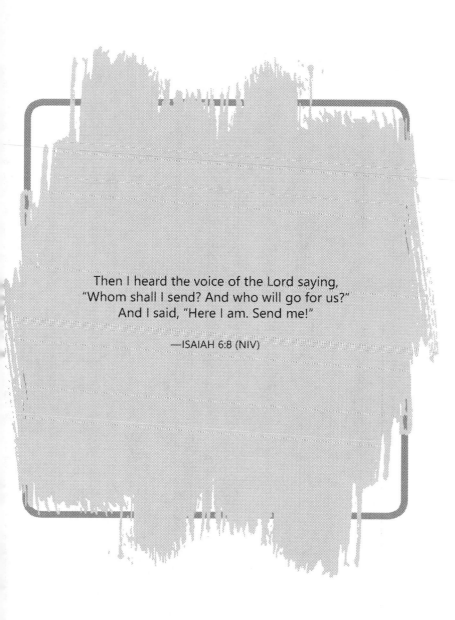

Then I heard the voice of the Lord saying,
"Whom shall I send? And who will go for us?"
And I said, "Here I am. Send me!"

—ISAIAH 6:8 (NIV)

*O*ver the course of my life, I've had so many experiences that I want to share. I feel I've written so much from a place of hurt and pain. The first couple of times I got started on this devotional, this story didn't make the cut. As I went back and looked over all the things I'd written, I realized I had to include this, and out of all the stories I could start with, I'm choosing this to start off with. Why? Life isn't about waiting for storms to pass; it's about learning to dance in the rain. Sometimes the most beautiful moments are the ones you can only encounter in the middle of a storm. Some of the greatest lessons come during the hardest pains. You will never be prepared for where God leads and calls you to. I pray that as you read this you have courage to step out of your comfort zone and take a chance. Allow God to move in and through you in an incredible way. Don't give up hope when something doesn't work out the way you hoped; instead, believe that God has a plan. His plans are greater than our dreams.

The rubber will meet the road soon, and I do not feel qualified. I'm suddenly terrified but secretly hoping this is God's plan. My heart is pounding with anticipation and fear. I doubt my abilities. I doubt God has some great plan for us. I doubt the answer will be yes. Even though I can't imagine any of this, I choose to believe that God calls the unqualified, and boy, is that the case. I choose to believe that, though I doubt, God created us to do more than just live. Though all the circumstances around us say this shouldn't work out, I choose to believe that God's plan and will are unimaginable. It's been a long road to get to where we are today. I secretly hope *this* is finally *the one*, but it's OK if it isn't. I've warned Him that I will fail Him, but I will fight to become better. I choose to believe through the fear, through the doubt, and through the unknown that God is in control. I trust and believe in Him. His plan and His will will prevail. God, I will trust you—even if the answer is no. I will praise you even if the answer is not yet, not this one. With my arms wide open and my heart abandoned, I will trust you because your plan is greater than all my fears and my ideas. Will you?

Repeat these words until you find the peace of God today:

> *I will trust you, even if the answer is no. I will praise you even if the answer is not yet, not this one. With my arms wide open and my heart abandoned, I will trust you because your plan is greater than all my fears and my ideas.*

My hope and prayer is that if you find yourself in situations where you feel unqualified, remember that God may be using this to grow you and your faith. If you felt qualified and knew exactly what to do, then you may not rely on God to help you do it.

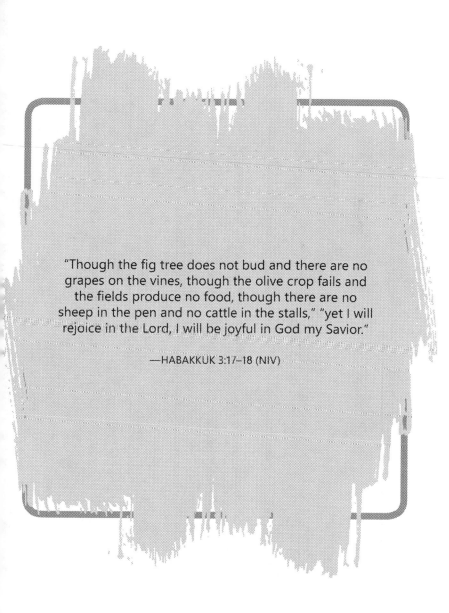

"Though the fig tree does not bud and there are no grapes on the vines, though the olive crop fails and the fields produce no food, though there are no sheep in the pen and no cattle in the stalls," "yet I will rejoice in the Lord, I will be joyful in God my Savior."

—HABAKKUK 3:17–18 (NIV)

Thope this inspires you today to keep moving! Keep pressing on, even when you feel like you have nothing left. When you think your story is over, God is here to say your story is just beginning. God is here and ready to do amazing things. Put down your pen and allow Him to write the story He created you for. He will never leave nor forsake you. You just have to let go and allow him to move. Fight the darkness until His morning light comes.

I know how hard it is to listen, to believe He is here. Trust me, I have asked Him. I've actually yelled at Him, asking where He was in the darkness. Where was He in that moment when I was desperately needing Him? I have been in places I didn't think I'd make it out of—in places where I couldn't see how loved I was or where I just wanted my pain to be over or places where living another day seemed too much to bear.

I can't tell you how many times I've driven down the road and thought about driving into the side of a bridge. This wasn't during a time I was an unbeliever; it was actually quite the opposite. I went to church every Sunday and Wednesday, went to my church's small group meetings, and listened to nothing but Christian radio. Friend, when I tell you that finding hope in the darkness isn't easy, I don't tell you that because I can't relate. I tell you because I have had to fight this darkness my entire life. Hang on, and don't give up.

Find one thing, one person, one truth, one saying to cling to with all the fibers of your being. This small hope can slowly make the darkness fade into the night.

My hope and prayer when the darkness comes is that you will remember you are not alone. Begin to speak the name of Jesus. When you can't, He will. Ask Him to come in this moment with you. He's here waiting.

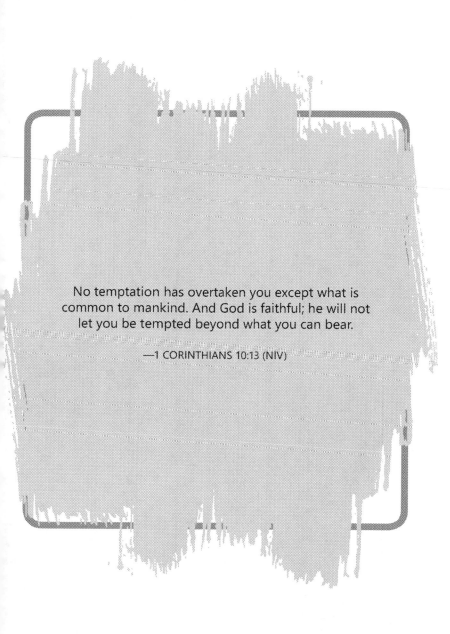

No temptation has overtaken you except what is common to mankind. And God is faithful; he will not let you be tempted beyond what you can bear.

—1 CORINTHIANS 10:13 (NIV)

*L*ife experiences can lead you to a point of such brokenness that you're left standing alone, empty and directionless when you've given every part of yourself to God and somehow find yourself in the middle of nowhere, numb. You're numb because you've cried all tears you can cry, because you've fallen down on your knees and given Him everything that you have, and because you've prayed for hours and days for God to not only move in your life, but your husband's, your family's, your kids', your business's, and your friends' lives. You're numb after years of serving Him with constant battles of the mind and heart, because you desperately want to give your family 100 percent of you, but you don't have the energy.

You're full of guilt and shame because you can never get time back. You set out with the best intentions but ended up angry at yourself because you messed up again. You're depressed about your current situation because you've done everything you know to do and yet you're standing in the middle of a crowded room with signs all around pointing you in the direction you need to go, and you're still lost. So you just stand there. Life around you keeps going. Everyone's laughing and smiling. Dreams are coming true, people are being healed, miracles are being performed, and you're just *there*. Your mind and heart are blank. You just *exist*. The next thing happens. Then your child gets sick and you watch them suffer or that dream opportunity gets crushed (for literally the hundredth time) or the bank account's empty. The joy is gone, and you're exhausted mentally, physically, and emotionally. You are on the edge. Can it get worse? Absolutely.

Your health and your husband's health suffer, costing extra money that you don't have on doctor visits, medicine, CT-scans, and possible surgery. The list keeps going. The trials get harder, the pain gets deeper, and the tears flow harder. *Why?* I so desperately want to have an answer for you, but I don't. There will be so many moments in your life when there will be more whys than answers. I don't know your why, but I can tell you, looking back over my life, my story, my pain, and my darkness, I truly believe it's all part of God's plan for my life. Though I think that may be why, it doesn't make it easier. It doesn't make it better.

I pray that as you read this you find hope. I pray you find comfort in knowing you aren't alone. I know it's hard. When you are going through the fire, you can't see past the flames. It's only when you make it through that you can see even in this. He is here, and He is faithful. It's so easy to miss the goodness of God if we don't take time to remember the moments we never thought we'd make it out of. Take a deep breath, and believe you can make it through this too.

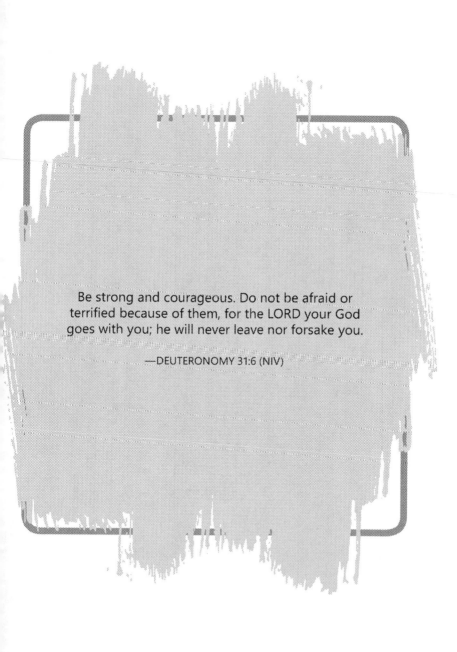

Be strong and courageous. Do not be afraid or
terrified because of them, for the LORD your God
goes with you; he will never leave nor forsake you.

—DEUTERONOMY 31:6 (NIV)

ometimes it feels like one more thing turns into a thousand things. When it seems like there can't possibly be anything else, then something else happens. You find yourself wanting to give up. You just can't take it anymore. So how do you keep going when you feel like you can't?

When these moments come for me, I honestly don't want to fight. I want to give up and live selfishly. I don't want to care about anyone else or dream of helping others; I am tired of it all. I want to be selfish. I want to be selfish for once and maybe I am a little, but I can't. This will be one of the most "churchy" answers I will ever give you, but it's the one truth I desperately want you to hear: *It's not about us.* It's about God. It's about the purpose God created us for.

God leads us to be examples to others so that we don't let them wonder, but instead teach them about how to love like Jesus. We show how to give when we have nothing to give and keep fighting even when we're numb to show others they are worthy. Only then can they know how to show still more people that they are worthy too. We show unconditional love so they can love others unconditionally, and we teach them there's more to life than status, class, the car you have, the house you live in, and so on. Life isn't about the material things we acquire, but about the lives we can touch with a smile, a hello, a helping hand, or by loving the "unlovable."

So I'll keep fighting even when I want to give up. I will keep fighting even when it's painful. I pray you find strength to keep fighting even when you don't see the purpose. Just keep fighting. I pray for the one who is waiting. I pray for the one who's on the verge of new beginnings. I pray for the one who's fighting to keep the small flicker of hope still alive. I pray for the one whose journey is just beginning and for the one who feels like she's drowning and tomorrow seems too far away. I pray for the one who is scared. For the one who seems like this darkness will never end, I'm praying for you.

I can't tell you that what's on the other side will be all you dreamed of or that you'll definitely be super successful. I can't tell you you'll go to bed not feeling hopeless. But what I can tell you is that you need to find a truth and cling to it. Remember a time when you thought you wouldn't make it out of a situation, but God showed up and delivered you. Remember a time you didn't think you had the funds, but it turned out you had just what you needed (not what you wanted, what you needed). God is here. God hears you. God is faithful—even when it's hard to believe.

Trust that if God brought you through that thing, He will bring you through this thing as well. If God provided then, He will provide now. Take a deep breath, and grasp with all your might the knowledge that God has you in the palms of his hands.

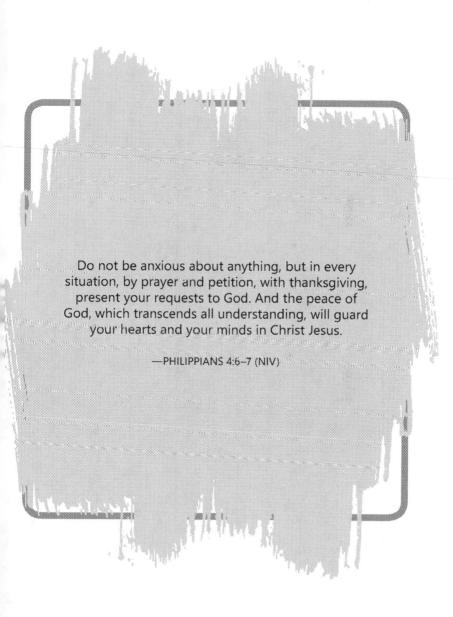

Do not be anxious about anything, but in every situation, by prayer and petition, with thanksgiving, present your requests to God. And the peace of God, which transcends all understanding, will guard your hearts and your minds in Christ Jesus.

—PHILIPPIANS 4:6–7 (NIV)

Sometimes a small, broken, faint whisper to an indescribable Emanuel is all you need. Life isn't easy nor perfect, but God is faithful and loving. Be still and know He is God. Allow this to sink into your soul today. Sometimes all it takes is a whisper of His name to quiet a soul. With your eyes closed, take a deep breath and whisper, *Jesus*. Keep doing this for as long as you need. He's there waiting to meet you.

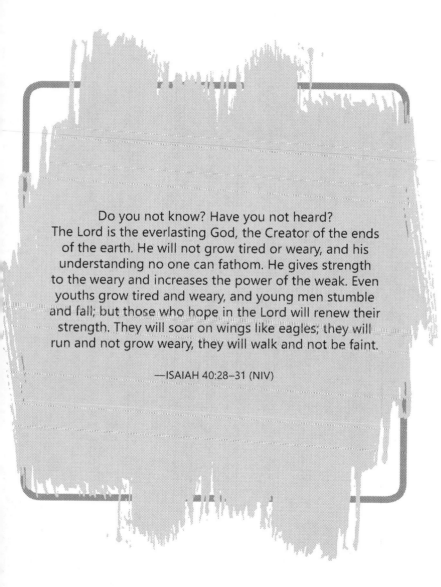

Do you not know? Have you not heard?
The Lord is the everlasting God, the Creator of the ends
of the earth. He will not grow tired or weary, and his
understanding no one can fathom. He gives strength
to the weary and increases the power of the weak. Even
youths grow tired and weary, and young men stumble
and fall; but those who hope in the Lord will renew their
strength. They will soar on wings like eagles; they will
run and not grow weary, they will walk and not be faint.

—ISAIAH 40:28–31 (NIV)

I've asked and prayed, and yet, nothing. I've tried so hard to be faithful, to believe and hope when I felt like giving up, and yet, nothing. Others seem to get what they want and have dreams come true, and yet here I sit, mentally, physically, and emotionally exhausted with no more hope and no time for dreams. I've struggled with feeling like I matter. It's always seemed to me that others mattered more, that their hopes and dreams mattered more than mine do. I've prayed and sought earnestly for where you want me to go and what you want me to do.

Really? You knew my struggle was getting harder and harder and that the battle was becoming stronger each day I walked, and yet, nothing. You did nothing. Why? *I was fine!*

How do you keep going and fighting when it feels like the darkness has you in a perpetual state of fog? The fog is so strong that you can barely breathe, much less know that you need to fight. You hang on. You take one breath at a time. For me, this was the moment I really had to start just saying the name *Jesus.* As I began to say *Jesus* to myself, peace began to fill my mind, and I could see enough to fight a little harder. I moved from where I was sitting. I took some deep breaths and realized I needed to text someone to distract my mind. In the moment I spoke His name, He came. He gave me the peace I needed to get through that moment.

My friend, I pray that when you don't know what else to do, you begin to speak the name *Jesus,* and He will come.

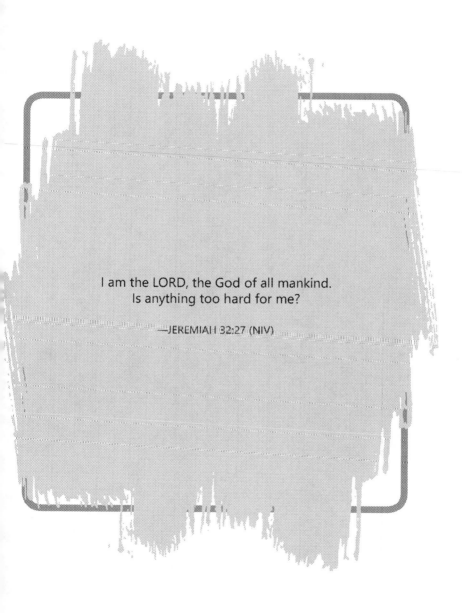

I am the LORD, the God of all mankind.
Is anything too hard for me?

—JEREMIAH 32:27 (NIV)

*W*hen you're waiting, seconds can seem like minutes, minutes can seem like hours, and days can feel like weeks or months. It's frustrating, and it's *hard* to wait! I often doubt I will ever truly learn patience.

I want to control situations so badly. It's *hard* to sit back and allow God to keep control. I am thankful I can look back and see how I've grown in this area, but I am nowhere near close to being good at it. It's ridiculously hard for me to wait. I need an answer; I need a solution; I need to fix it.

Allowing God to be in control is difficult. I'm not kidding when I say I have to remind myself every five minutes that God's got this. It's His will, not ours. It's His timing, not mine.

I want to encourage you to hang on no matter the situation or how far you feel from God. No matter how impossible the situation seems, God is in control. The situation may not end how you imagined or wanted it to, but God has a purpose for all things. We may not like, see, or understand, but we really don't need to. We just need to believe that God's got this, and God has *you*.

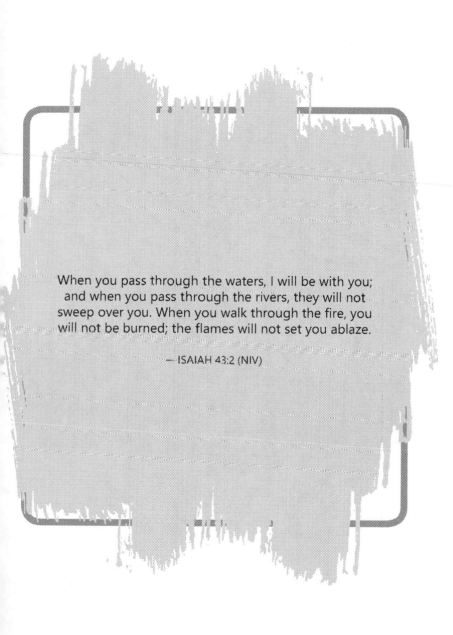

When you pass through the waters, I will be with you;
and when you pass through the rivers, they will not
sweep over you. When you walk through the fire, you
will not be burned; the flames will not set you ablaze.

— ISAIAH 43:2 (NIV)

Ⅰn 2016 I realized there had to be a greater purpose for me than just being surrounded by my office walls day in and day out, never talking to anyone. That couldn't possibly be all God had planned for every experience in my life up to that moment. Since that realization, I've learned a lot about who I am and who I was created to be. I've been learning how to live for God.

I'm learning to love myself. I'm learning that I can't do everything for everyone. I'm learning to speak more softly, respond less quickly, and let go more. I'm learning to seek God's will before my own. I'm learning to not only tell my husband and kids I love them, but *show* them I do. I'm learning how to let go of the control I want to have on our lives and giving it to God. I'm learning how to put the pen down and concentrate on not picking it back up. I'm learning to trust God more. I'm learning to listen and hear His quiet voice. I'm learning how to make the most of the moments I have.

I'm learning to trust God's timing. I'm learning to trust God's plan. I'm learning how to believe in myself. I'm learning not to compare myself with others. I'm learning how to control my anger. I'm learning how to let go of pain. I'm learning how to live without my dad. I'm learning how to draw closer to God, even when I feel abandoned. I'm learning how to not give up. I'm learning how to keep fighting, even when I feel hopeless. I'm learning how to get out of my comfort zone. I'm learning to lose myself in order to become who God created me to be. I'm learning to live purposefully.

I open my heart in the hope it might help you. Maybe it inspires you. Maybe you can see that you're not alone. Maybe it reminds you that, even in the tears and pain, there's still hope. Maybe you can see God has a plan and purpose for your life. Maybe you can see you're loved beyond measure. Maybe you see it's OK to not be OK—just don't stay there. Find the strength to keep fighting and keep believing. God loves you too.

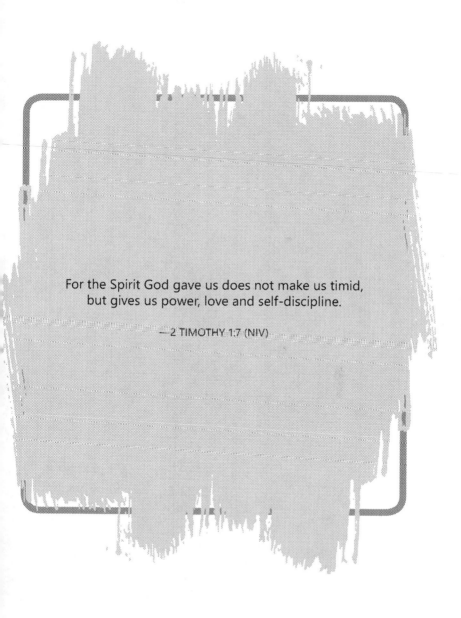

For the Spirit God gave us does not make us timid,
but gives us power, love and self-discipline.

—2 TIMOTHY 1:7 (NIV)

*H*ave you ever stopped to wonder whether you aren't actually waiting on God, but instead God's been waiting on you? Have you been asking God *why*? Why hasn't He opened the door? Why hasn't He changed your situation? Why hasn't He answered your prayer?

One day during a lunch break I decided to eat on our back porch. I wondered why God hadn't moved, why my current situation was still the same. God could've opened a door, but he hadn't. I looked up and noticed a tree in our yard. It had obviously been in our yard long before we'd moved in, but I'd never noticed it before. It seemed slim and unnoticeable, yet it stuck out like a sore thumb.

I left my house and headed back to work, just dumbfounded that I'd noticed this tree at this moment. I searched for why I'd noticed that tree at that moment and realized I was no longer happy with the life I was living. I realized every time God answered my prayers the way I wanted, they turned out not to be as amazing as I'd expected. I realized that day I was created for a purpose far greater than just living. I was created for more than going to work and then home— for more than sitting in my office, never leaving until I got off.

These realizations, along with every pain, tear, joy, decision, mistake, and step has led me to a deeper relationship with God. I've spent the last two years trying desperately to seek God's will and plan and *not* what I think I want.

The job I prayed for, dreamed of, and finally got turned out not to be as great as I'd hoped. A new boss came in, and suddenly the whole atmosphere changed to something I didn't want to be a part of. Each day I became unhappier. I was becoming a person I didn't recognize. I struggled so much, knowing God could change it and didn't. I kept waiting, but nothing happened.

On a random day, while speaking with my husband he said, "If you want to leave, I'm OK with that. If you're unhappy, then leave. I've already told you this, and this is the last time I'm going to say it.

We'll make it work if you want to leave. So do you want to stay, or do you want to leave?"

In the moment I admitted wanting to leave, something broke inside me. I realized God had just been waiting on me to move. I hadn't been waiting on Him; He'd been waiting on me. He was waiting for me to make the decision to leave before He could open the doors for the next step. I had to be willing to let go of control and trust Him to work everything out.

Have you stopped and asked yourself whether God has been waiting on you to take the next step? Once upon a time I considered staying home, but ultimately that wasn't a life I wanted. So it wasn't a thought that *ever* truly crossed my mind. Even in the midst of a very stressful ongoing situation, I always found an excuse. When God has a plan for your life, there's *nothing* that can stop it except you.

For two years I chose to stay, until staying became the one option I could not and would not accept anymore. I was hurt and angry. I felt I shouldn't have been the one leaving. I shouldn't have had to make the choice between staying or going. But I chose to leave. I chose to alter our families' lives. That's a heavy burden I still carry. When I walked out the doors, I walked out knowing that step was the right one. I took a deep breath and let go of it all.

Stepping into the unknown is scary, and I can't say it's been easy. I can definitely say it's been worth it though. God is able and can do anything, but you have to speak the word. You have to make the decision. You have to let go and trust Him. The choice is yours. You have to be willing to let go and let God's will be done in and through your life.

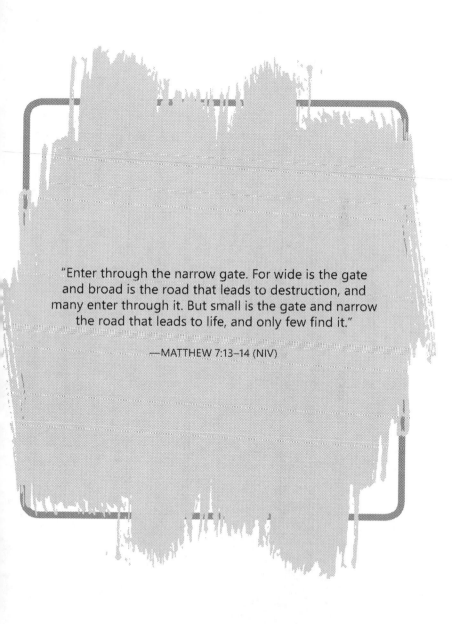

"Enter through the narrow gate. For wide is the gate and broad is the road that leads to destruction, and many enter through it. But small is the gate and narrow the road that leads to life, and only few find it."

—MATTHEW 7:13–14 (NIV)

*O*n a random day on the way to the boutique we owned, I felt God say it was time to sell our business. We knew God opened the door in 2018 for us to buy this boutique, but now God was saying it was time to sell a place I so deeply loved and enjoyed every day. It was time for me to take a step back and support my husband. This was March 11—just four days before not only our lives would be shattered, but the world. There couldn't have been a worse time to try to sell a business. In July of 2019 we finally officially listed our business for sale, not because it was failing or wasn't making money, but because God had other plans for us.

Day after day I went to work, knowing that God had said to sell, and yet it hadn't sold. Along came three buyers, each of which are long stories by themselves. I think I'd reached my breaking point of things I could handle by this time. These three failed offers just added onto the past six years of trial after trial. I was giving up. I just could not take it anymore. I honestly couldn't fight. This thought came to mind, and I thought just maybe there was someone out there who, like me, could use this inspiration.

If given the choice to go back down the same road traveled, I've always believed I'd choose the same road again, even if it's difficult and ends in loss— even if it's painful and full of tears, anger, and whys. I firmly believe God has a plan and a purpose for everything under the sun. Though I don't always know or understand, I trust Him and His purpose; however, the other day I asked myself whether I'd really choose this road again based on my circumstances in that moment. For the first time I thought I might not have. I tried so hard to convince myself I would, but in that moment of total despair, hurt, and confusion, I would've chosen to pray different prayers that didn't lead me to where I was.

Why? That's a great question, and I'm not sure I completely understand my own thought. But I know I wouldn't want to go through all the ups and down over that month. I wouldn't have wanted to come so close to what seemed like answered prayers and unbelievable dreams coming true to only have them crushed, not once, but twice in the same month. I've probably experienced worse, but right then the mental battle seemed relentless. I was just too exhausted. I knew I'd heard God, so why was I still there? I'd experienced defeat and letdowns before, but this one left me crushed, defeated, and questioning. I truly wanted to give up. I just couldn't understand why.

Sometimes in life you take unexpected detours to find yourself in most difficult places. To say I've struggled over the years is an understatement. It's been so incredibly hard. It's been emotionally, physically, and most definitely mentally draining and exhausting. I've fought battles that no one's seen or knows about. But today, I realized that I'm exactly where I needed to be, I wouldn't be the person I am right now in this moment writing this had it not been for that moment. I couldn't see in that moment the greater purpose in my struggles. I couldn't see in that moment that the path I may not have chosen again led me to a place I've dreamed of for so long.

I pray when you don't know if you'd choose the same path, the same trials, the same hurt, that you remember this story and find inspiration. There is a purpose for this too. I pray that you find comfort in knowing I'm not perfect. My life's a mess. I don't have it together. I doubt and struggle every day.

I pray you find your ember and cling to it for dear life. I pray that no matter how you think your world is swirling out of control you have peace, even if only for a moment. God, I pray you will forgive us and help us and our numbness.

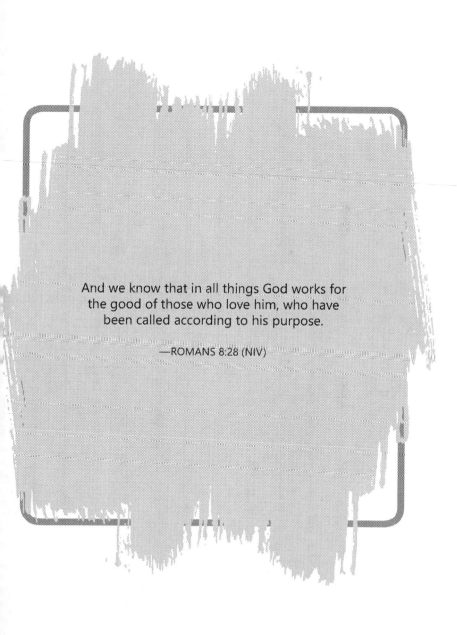

And we know that in all things God works for the good of those who love him, who have been called according to his purpose.

—ROMANS 8:28 (NIV)

There are a thousand things I want to say, but honestly I have no words. I can't begin to imagine what others are feeling tonight. I can't begin to imagine the questions, the whys, or the soul-ache you must be feeling. I don't have any advice or encouraging words. There's nothing I can say or do to make this any easier or less painful. But I can say it's OK to be broken. It's OK to be angry. It's OK to be in shock. It's OK to feel hopeless.

I can't promise you everything will be OK. I can't tell you that holding onto the promises of God will be easy. However, I can tell you that you may have doubts. You may always wonder why. You may always question whether you could have done more. You may always wonder if you prayed hard enough or had enough faith. You may even wonder, *If God is good, then why?* I can tell you that you will have good days, and you'll have days when nothing seems to matter and it's hard to imagine ever laughing again. The world will continue to spin, and it will seem as though no one cares or even notices the pain you feel. When you do laugh or smile you may feel guilty, and that may never really go away.

Eventually you will be OK. It's not going to be tomorrow or even next year. It may take two, five, or even ten years, but you will be OK. The pain you feel will get better, but it never goes away. Someday you'll find the strength to let go, and it's going to be OK. The devil will try to make you feel ashamed and guilty, and as hard as it is to see past this, you shouldn't. There's a long emotional journey ahead of you.

Each day will have a new emotion, a reminder, and more questions than answers. God already knows how you feel. Don't hold back or hold it in. Fall on your knees and scream if you need to. Punch a pillow, but most importantly, cry like you've never cried before. Allow the pain to overcome you completely. This won't make things better or change anything, but your soul needs to grieve. Your soul needs to remember. This helps preserve the memories, not only in your mind, but in your soul. If I could tell you one thing it would be to cling to God with every fiber of your being.

You know all about the goodness and promises of God, but those are probably just empty words right now. That's OK! I wish I could take your pain away. I wish I could bring you comfort, but I can't; however, I can tell you that you are loved more than you can imagine. I can tell you that you did nothing to deserve this. Jesus died so you could live. I can't imagine how incredibly difficult this is for you, but this is not your fault. It's not the doctors', your husband's or wife's, your mom's, sister's, brother's, dad's, or God's fault. Yes, He allowed this to happen. Yes, He could have prevented it. Yes, there are others who didn't have this happen, and no, God doesn't love you less or them more.

I can't see God's plan. I can't see His reasoning, and I definitely can't comprehend how and why this happened, but I do believe that God has a purpose and a plan for every smile, for every laugh, for every tear, for every pain, and most importantly, for every life.

Sweet friend, my heart hurts for you. I'm praying for you. When you don't have the strength to stand, kneel. When the pain is too much to speak, let your tears be the words of your heart. It's hard! But I pray you always remember that God loves you. He will be the strength you need to make it. You won't always feel him near, but He will never leave you. You are surrounded by people who love you and want to help you through this. You may not want to speak, but our shoulders are here. Our ears are open to just listening—even to the same questions or the same whys. There are no judgments—only open arms with open hearts to help in whatever ways we can.

I pray for peace and comfort as you face the uncertainties that lie ahead.

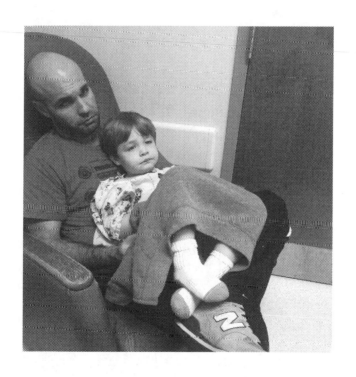

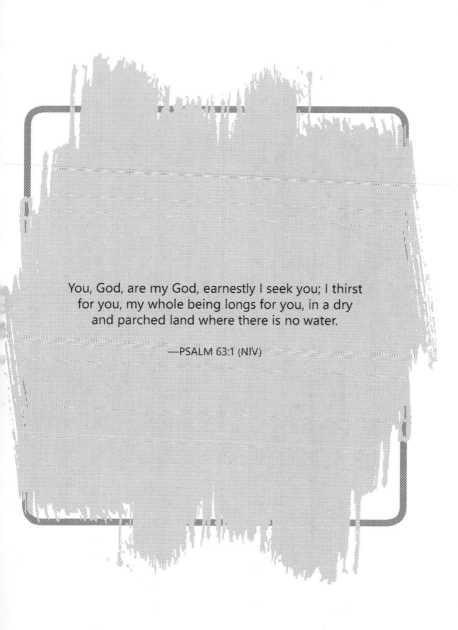

You, God, are my God, earnestly I seek you; I thirst for you, my whole being longs for you, in a dry and parched land where there is no water.

—PSALM 63:1 (NIV)

I 've written this a thousand times in my head, and yet I still have no idea what to say. I'm struggling—not that *that's* anything new. I find myself battling internally because I need a miracle. I need prayers, but I feel horrible because I know there are others who need to see and feel God more than I do. My situation doesn't compare to the heartaches, the roller-coaster rides, the sleepless nights, the wonderings that others will experience. My heart breaks for them, and my mind tries to remember to pray for them. But at the same time I want to be selfish and think about myself and my problems right now.

I think I'm being completely selfish by wanting to take time to pray for myself, but I honestly don't have the energy. It's a difficult time emotionally for me, which doesn't help my sanity or my current situation. So why tell you this? That's a great question that I can't answer. I'm just being honest. I'm not perfect, and I definitely don't have life or walking with God figured out. Right now I'm fighting with what very little energy I do have.

I know every answer out there you'd get at church. I know God's plans will come to pass, and I know it happens in His time. *I know He can!* I *know* that the only, *only* way is for *God Himself* to do a miracle. In times like this the only thing we can do is pray and believe it will all work out according to His plan in His time, but right now I'm tired of fighting my mind for control. I'm tired of trying to fight myself. I don't have the energy to care anymore. I'm tired of the mountain-top moments and endless nights in the valley. It's not supposed to be easy, but a break longer than a gust of wind would be nice.

To the girl who finds herself suddenly in a life she didn't choose, I know she's hurting, and even though she's determined not to, she secretly questions and wonders why she's where she is. While I want to be selfish and worry about my life and my kids, there are people all around us that need our love, support, and prayers. Sometimes we need to look around and be thankful for the blessings surrounding us. There are others who would love to be in our shoes. Yes, I do believe we need to pray for our lives and children, but we shouldn't be so consumed by those that we fail to pray for those around us. I also believe there are times in our lives when it's OK to just worry about ourselves. No, you don't have to get through your checklist of people. If you're just trying to survive right now, that's OK too.

Living for God isn't about checking all the boxes trying to be the perfect Christian or person. It's OK if we get mad. It's OK to take time to work through the trials of life. God already knows our thoughts and feelings. It's OK to be honest with him. It's OK! Just make sure you are praying and seeking God in these moments. Don't allow your current situation to rule your life. God is there and waiting to hear from you.

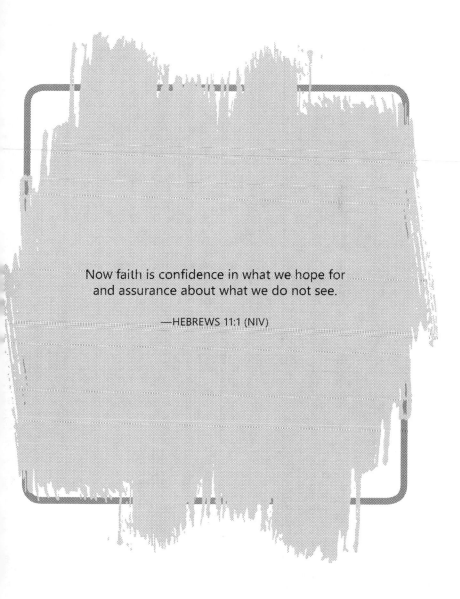

Now faith is confidence in what we hope for
and assurance about what we do not see.

—HEBREWS 11:1 (NIV)

We've been praying for a long time about something. It's hard to continue to have faith and believe when you can't see, feel, or hear God moving. The *truth* is that I've been wondering if God still performs miracles and answers prayers and whether He even loves me. Every day, for years, I've tried to do good and be good and do what I felt God was leading me to do, only to be left feeling frustrated, tired, and questioning it all.

I can't feel God moving. I can't see my prayers being answered. It's hard to believe God has other plans for us. It's hard to keep fighting when you see no reason to fight. Occasionally a door opens and you allow *hope* to fill your mind, only for it to lead absolutely nowhere. Once again you allowed yourself to believe that maybe, just maybe, this was the time God would hear your prayers, but *nope*. You're becoming better at not getting excited or allowing yourself to believe that this is the time. I've hardened my heart so that it doesn't get broken when I'm disappointed again. I honestly have no idea how I feel about this situation, but I do know I'm tired. I'm tired of it *all. I need and want* to *see God move!* I want to *see* miracles happen, to *see* lives changed. It's hard to believe when you have more questions than answers.

My friend, I'm here to tell you that God is still here. He's still in the prayer-answering business. He hasn't forgotten you. Just because you can't see Him working, it doesn't mean He's not. I don't know what today, tomorrow, next week, or next year holds. I do know that I *will* forget this, and I *will* question this. Why? Because I'm not perfect. I'm impatient. I like being in control of my situations, *but* in this moment I believe *God* is moving and working. I can't see it, *but I feel it.*

I have this peace about everything going wrong and right in our lives. I don't know what's going to happen, but that's OK!

When you can't see or feel God, you're not alone. I get it, but I pray that today this helps you find a little peace, even if it's only for a moment. God hasn't forgotten you. God hears you, and He's working, even when you can't see it.

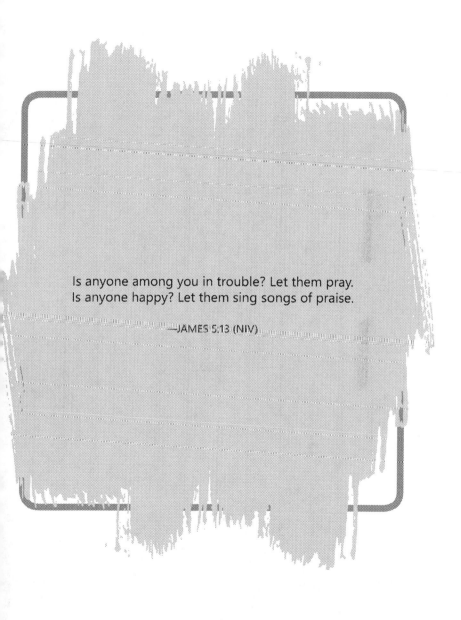

Is anyone among you in trouble? Let them pray.
Is anyone happy? Let them sing songs of praise.

—JAMES 5:13 (NIV)

I just want to encourage you today. Try to replace any negative thoughts in one of the following ways.

✧ If you are worried say aloud, "I trust you." Repeat these words until you start to feel the sweet peace of God.

✧ If you're scared say, "I trust you." Keep repeating these words until your fear turns to peace.

✧ If you feel like you're not good enough or that you'll never have a breakthrough, just keep saying, "Jesus, Jesus, Jesus, Jesus, I trust you." You were fearfully and wonderfully made and chosen by God. Repeat those words until the doubts melt away and peace surrounds your heart.

When your heart is hurting and the pain is too deep, start calling Jesus's name. He hears you, He sees you, He knows you're hurting, and He's waiting to comfort you.

Friends, I have been uttering these words nonstop. Doing so has allowed me to replace the negative thoughts, the questioning, and the wondering why with God's peace. I pray this helps break your negative thinking in the same way it has mine. I pray for peace and comfort for you today, sweet friends.

Sometimes we feel like we need these eloquent, well-thought-out prayers, but we don't. Jesus knows us better than we know ourselves. He knows the number of hairs on our heads. We don't need to know more or pray more eloquently for Him to hear us. My sweet friend, Jesus meets us right where we are—right in the middle of doubt and messy lives. He's just waiting for you to call Him. He's waiting to hear you say, "Jesus." Even though you have no idea where the journey will take you or how hard and painful tomorrow will be, you simply say, "I trust you."

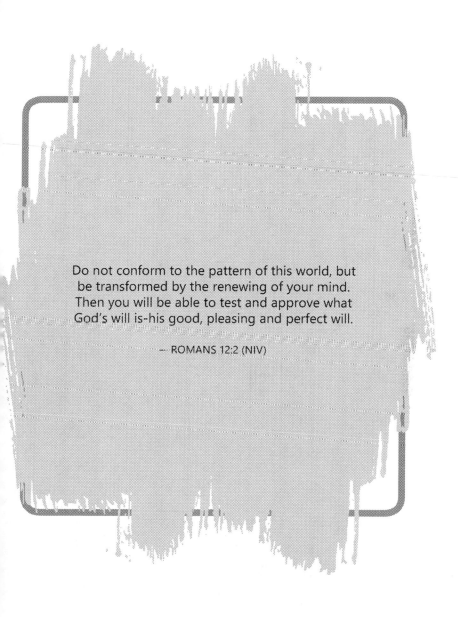

Do not conform to the pattern of this world, but
be transformed by the renewing of your mind.
Then you will be able to test and approve what
God's will is-his good, pleasing and perfect will.

— ROMANS 12:2 (NIV)

If you find yourself desperately wanting to change your circumstances—your marriage, your looks, your weight, your job, your life—it starts with you. Change doesn't come overnight, and it doesn't come easily. There's no magical pill, no magical solution, and no magical recipe. It's up to you and you alone. If you aren't happy, *you* have to do something to change it. It's not going to magically get better if you continue doing the same things over and over again. Just talking about eating healthier isn't the same as eating healthier. You actually *have to* eat healthier.

Is your marriage not what it used to be? Why? Have you looked inside your own heart to see whether there's something you can do to help it? Sometimes it's biting your tongue and not responding with what you want to say, but instead answering with humility to keep the peace. It's hard, but if we always respond from a place of anger and not from a place of peace, we will not have peace in our marriages.

You're getting older, and it's easier to gain weight. I get it— me too. But we're not going to take a magic pill or drink a magic coffee that will get us to stay at our healthiest weights for good. If you or I want to lose weight, it takes work. Instead of making excuses as to why we can't do something today, let's get up and start moving. It seems like it's so much easier to talk about why we can't do something, but actually it's not. We're just being lazy and using excuses.

If we truly stepped back and looked over our lives and areas that need improvement we would see that it starts with us, and more importantly, with our relationship to God. We've gotten so good at using being busy as an excuse. To be honest, if something is truly important to you, you will find a way to make time for it. It isn't ask, seek, knock. It's more than just saying words or making requests. It's when we make a request from our soul. It's when we seek with a pure heart to find, to desire, to obtain, and to search for something with an expectation of finding it. It's when we demolish barriers between walls.

My body isn't going to change if I continue doing nothing. I'm not going to lose weight if I eat anything and everything I want. I can make excuses and give a hundred reasons why I don't have time, but they're just that—excuses. If I truly wanted to make a change in my body, then I would find a way. Maybe someone says, "But it's so much easier to try magic pills, or try this diet or that diet." Why? Because committing to change takes time, dedication, and lots of hard work.

But I didn't decide to just change overnight. I didn't start working out overnight. It was a process that started with God. I prayed and explained how I felt guilty taking time away from the kids. I said how working all day and coming home to work out drained me so that I had no energy left for my husband. God slowly showed me I don't have to feel guilty for trying to improve my health. He opened my eyes to see opportunities to make time for working out while still having time for family.

I didn't do it. I can't do it. I need God! I need His guidance, His love, His mercy, and His grace. My friend, if you want to see changes in your life, your marriage, your career, and your circumstances, it's super simple—you make time for God! You ask God. You seek God. You knock on God's door. God will hear you. He will lead you. *But* you have to be willing to open your heart to what He has to say. You have to live the way He asks you to live. You have to surrender yourself and allow God to lead you, mold you, and shape you and your thinking.

I can't promise things will always work out how you want them to, but I can promise as long as you seek God and His will first, His plans will play out in your life. I promise His way will always be better than what you think. It may not be easy, it may not be quick, it may not be popular, and it will probably come with lots of tears, hard nights, and sad times, but a joy deep in your soul will come.

The peace will be the sweetest peace you've ever experienced. It may not be tomorrow. It probably won't be next week or next year, but one day it will happen! The first step starts with you.

I pray you find encouragement to know you're not alone in your thoughts. You're not alone in your unhappiness. You're not alone in loneliness. You're not alone with wanting a change, but you have no idea how to get there. If you do nothing else, decide today to start seeking God with all of you, not just a portion. If you can only spare all of you for one minute, then give him that one minute today. As you continue to give all of you each minute, the minute will turn to five minutes. Five minutes will turn to three minutes several times a day. It doesn't matter the amount of time; the intent of the heart is all that matters. Is the heart fully focused on God, or is half with God while half is on Facebook or talking to a friend or yelling at your child or fuming over the fight you had.

God is waiting to meet you where you are! Grow with God, and the rest will fall into place.

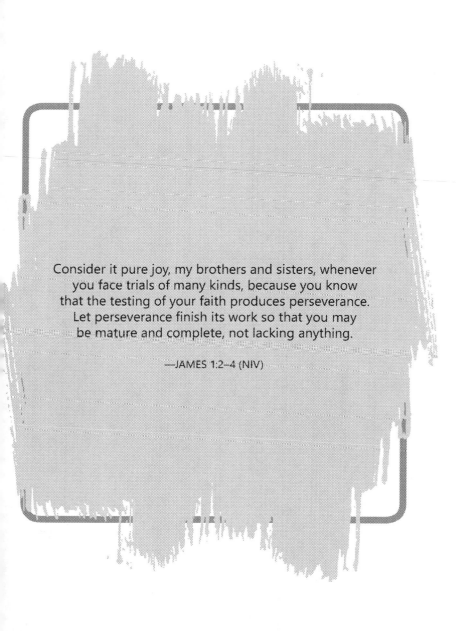

Consider it pure joy, my brothers and sisters, whenever
you face trials of many kinds, because you know
that the testing of your faith produces perseverance.
Let perseverance finish its work so that you may
be mature and complete, not lacking anything.

—JAMES 1:2–4 (NIV)

S ometimes life seems like a flood. It's not just one thing; it's a thousand things. These are the days when it's one step forward and three steps back, when if it's not the broken air-conditioner, it's the tires that need replacing. The light bill is doubling, and the kids need new clothes for school or supplies for some extracurricular activity. There can never be *just one thing*. What fun would that be?

It's through these endless *things* that we learn our most important lessons. It's where we grow—or at least should—in our relationships with God. How we respond is what will make or crush our days. We can choose to let the flood ruin our day and impact everything else we do negatively, *or* we can choose to smile. Will smiling stop the flood? Nope! Will smiling prevent the next thing? Nope! So why smile?

Smiling will allow God in. Smiling will allow God to move. Smiling will allow you to have a day with at least one less thing to feel guilty about. Why? When we are mad, frustrated, angry, sad, or hurting, those feelings project negatively on everything and everyone around us. We don't mean for it to; it just does. When we choose to smile, we are choosing joy in sorrow. We are choosing happiness in the sadness. We are choosing not to allow the things we can't control to control us. Each day we will face new challenges. Each day we will have a choice. Each day we are given the opportunity to seek or ignore God. Each day has a lesson to learn and a choice to grow or sit idle. So today, will you choose to smile?

When you choose to smile God can do amazing things in and through you.

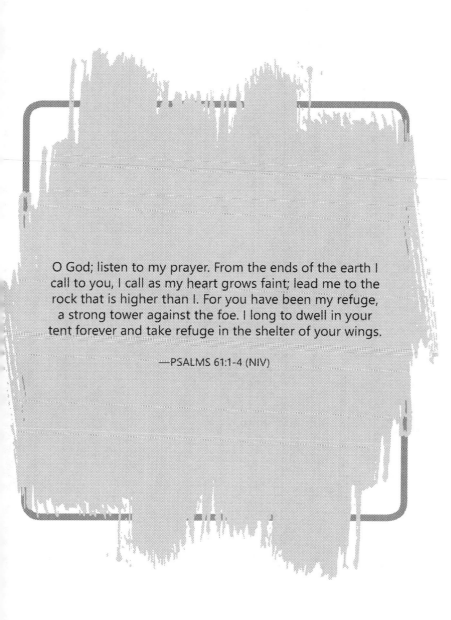

O God; listen to my prayer. From the ends of the earth I call to you, I call as my heart grows faint; lead me to the rock that is higher than I. For you have been my refuge, a strong tower against the foe. I long to dwell in your tent forever and take refuge in the shelter of your wings.

—PSALMS 61:1-4 (NIV)

*O*h my, I remember backing out of my parking spot at GSU wondering, *What's happening? What's going on? Why does it seem like I'm falling apart? God, why is everything falling apart? I thought I was where you wanted me to be, doing what you wanted me to do, being who you wanted me to be, and yet it's all falling apart.*

If you haven't noticed, I question myself, and I question my faith. I question God often—not because I don't have faith or don't believe, but because I'm human. My tendency is to lean on my understanding—or lack thereof. I can only see what my human eyes perceive. My heart is shattered by experiences, so I can't see what God sees. I cannot know what God knows, and sometimes it's hard to live by faith and not by sight. So I question, wonder, and sometimes yell, but I try to always find my way back to God.

Sometimes I get frustrated because I just want to wallow in self-pity and doubt, so finding God again and getting my mind to focus on Him is very difficult. It seems I'm so lost in the darkness of my mind that I'll never come out, but eventually the darkness fades away and I'm reminded I'm not broken. I'm not a puzzle slowly being put back together. I'm slowly becoming who God created me to be.

So in this moment, remember you are loved! You are worthy! You are wanted! You are enough! Your world isn't falling apart; it's falling into place. God is here, and he's waiting on you. He will be here when you're ready. He loves you, my friend.

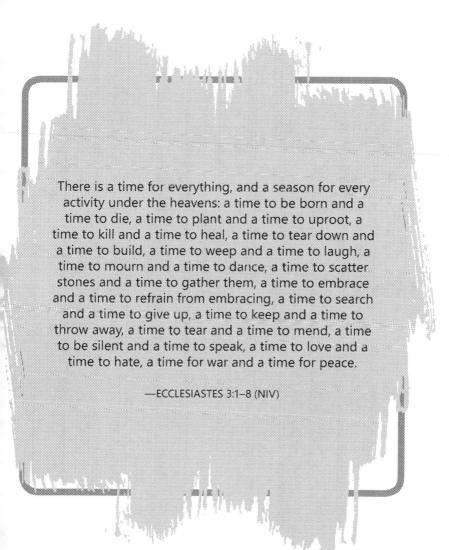

There is a time for everything, and a season for every activity under the heavens: a time to be born and a time to die, a time to plant and a time to uproot, a time to kill and a time to heal, a time to tear down and a time to build, a time to weep and a time to laugh, a time to mourn and a time to dance, a time to scatter stones and a time to gather them, a time to embrace and a time to refrain from embracing, a time to search and a time to give up, a time to keep and a time to throw away, a time to tear and a time to mend, a time to be silent and a time to speak, a time to love and a time to hate, a time for war and a time for peace.

—ECCLESIASTES 3:1–8 (NIV)

I clearly remember the day this message sank into my soul, and I finally realized that God's plan was far greater than what I could have imagined. I know this, I lived this, and I experienced this, but even though I did, I find myself back in what seems like a my-plan moment. I know God opens doors, but were these the doors God had meant to open? Or had He opened the doors to *my* plans to teach me another lesson so that I'd learn to lean into Him and trust Him more?

We've all had days that were great, when we really tried to live, love, and be who God called us to be, but there will be days when we don't. And that's OK too! There's always a lesson we can learn, even in moments when we believe our way is better. So if you're like me and have found yourself in a place you thought would be glorious but turned out nothing like you envisioned—it's OK! Don't feel guilty. Don't beat yourself up over making a mistake.

Dig deep, look around, and ask God what the lesson is this season that will help you grow more deeply into the person He created you to be. Ask! Seek! Knock! When we come surrendered, with an open heart and grateful mind, He will hear us! He will answer us. He is the God of perfect timing!

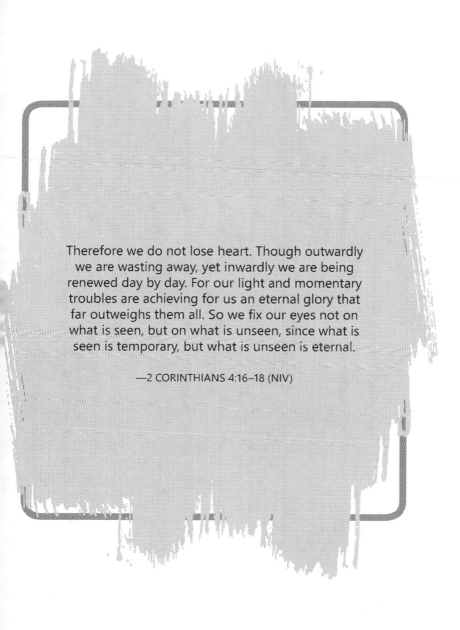

Therefore we do not lose heart. Though outwardly we are wasting away, yet inwardly we are being renewed day by day. For our light and momentary troubles are achieving for us an eternal glory that far outweighs them all. So we fix our eyes not on what is seen, but on what is unseen, since what is seen is temporary, but what is unseen is eternal.

—2 CORINTHIANS 4:16–18 (NIV)

Today I should've been celebrating my dad's sixty-ninth birthday. Instead he's celebrating with Jesus, and I'm left here behind, trying to hold myself together. Over the last thirteen birthdays, each one has hit differently. This year, as the months and days were counting down, I knew this one was going to hit a little harder than usual. I honestly had no idea why this would be the case—maybe it's because I've been by his grave more this year than I had in any previous year. I never go there, because it's too hard, but when your job requires you to, it's kind of hard not to look, not to stop, not to get out. Maybe it's because we are experiencing a time in our history unlike we ever have before. The truth is that I have no explanation, just emotions.

I didn't want to be alone in a building where my thoughts would run rampant or drive for fifty minutes alone with nothing but time to think about how much I was hurting. Twenty-five years with him will never have been enough time. Every second without him will always be a second too long. Losing someone you love never gets easier. The pain never truly goes away. I still cry when I see a dad with his little girl. I cry watching James with our little girl.

I deal with my pain by not thinking about it. Is that right? No, but that's what allows me to get up each day and appear to the world to be OK. While I am OK, that doesn't mean I'm not still hurting, broken, and questioning. It just means I've learned how to deal with all the feelings better. It's OK to not be OK. It's OK to cry. It's OK to hurt. It's OK to let go every once in a while, but remember to just not stay that way. We can't stop our pain or hurting forever; that's definitely not good. It's OK to laugh, smile, and go a day without thinking about the person we so desperately wish was with us. Don't feel guilty! Your body and soul need a rest from aching. In order to heal, to move forward, and to grow in our relationships with God.

I'm still learning each day how to live without my dad. I'm still learning that allowing life to move forward isn't something to be ashamed of or feel guilty about. I'm still growing in my relationship, but I frequently still question why. It doesn't make me a bad person or less of a believer—it's actually helping me grow. I know God has a reason and a purpose for everything, but that doesn't make it easier. It helps me work through the battles the devil keeps sending my way. It's a battle that God has already won. Sometimes it's so hard to fight past your thoughts, but I pray you keep fighting. God has already won. Keep telling the devil he can go back to hell. God is on the throne. He will not have power or control over you. He will not use this pain, this hurt, this loss to beat you down. God is here ready to rescue you! Just whisper his name.

If you can't find any other words then just whisper, "Jesus," over and over again. If you muster the strength, then just start saying, "Thank you, Jesus!" God hears our cries. He sees our tears. He knows and feels our brokenness. If you find yourself, like me, missing someone today or missing the idea of someone, I pray you find comfort in the arms of Jesus. Sometimes it feels like we are a thousand miles apart and he's nowhere to be found, but trust me, He's here! He's waiting. His arms are wrapped around you while you're struggling to take that next breath, that next step, to make that next day.

He is here! He loves you! How am I so sure? Because you, my friend, are reading this.

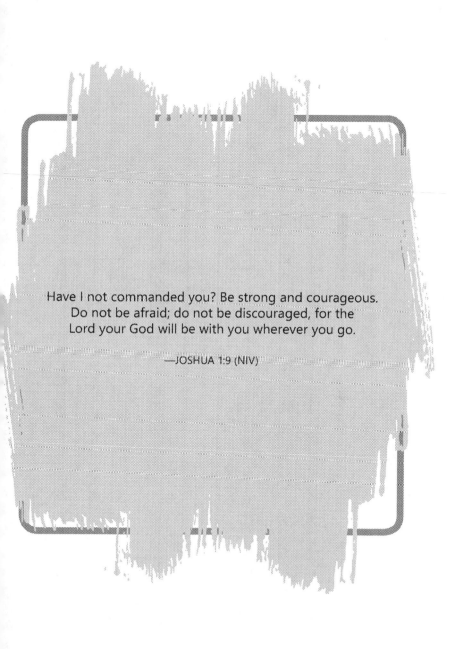

Have I not commanded you? Be strong and courageous.
Do not be afraid; do not be discouraged, for the
Lord your God will be with you wherever you go.

—JOSHUA 1:9 (NIV)

or the first time in a long time, I like the person I see in the mirror. She's worked hard! She's cried a lot of rivers, and she's carried secrets that no one will ever know. She's fought battles in her mind she didn't think would ever end. She's stronger on most days than she will ever believe. She's braver than anyone will ever know. She walks with her head held high and a smile brightly displayed on her face, but behind the outwardly beautiful, all-together woman, is a girl who's lost, hurting, and broken inside, but you'd never know or hear that from her.

She faces her fears on a daily basis. She is terrified to talk to people. She compares herself daily to those around her. She compares her successes and failures to those she sees as more successful, prettier, and more skilled than she. She doesn't think she's worthy of much of anything. She cries quietly in bed so no one hears or knows she's struggling. She never knew how much loving someone else could hurt even more until her babies were hurting. She's never felt more helpless than when she knows her babies are suffering and there's absolutely nothing she can do.

She's strong! She's fearless. She's brave. She's broken. She's lost. She's hurting. She is who she is today because of the experiences and lessons God has allowed in her life. She hasn't gotten to where she sits now because of who she is or what she's done, but because of God alone. We all make choices in each moment of our life. We can choose to be happy. We can choose to be free. We can choose to allow the pain, the hurts, and the brokenness to consume us, or we can choose to give God control. We can choose to allow him to mold us, shape us, and form us into the beautiful people we were created to be, or we can just exist. We can just survive. We can just live.

I'm telling you this to let you know that God sees you. He sees your pain and hears your cries. He hasn't forgotten you. He's waiting for you to open your heart and allow Him to wipe away your tears. Allow Him to heal your hurt. Allow Him to put the broken pieces back together. God sees her, but more importantly, God sees *you*! I don't know about you, but I've been asking where God is. Where is God in my pain? Where is God in my loss? Where is God in my loneliness? Where is God in the middle of this unimaginable fight? Where is God in my bitterness? Where is God in my unforgiveness?

I was asking God these exact questions when I looked up to the sky, and for the first time that I can ever clearly remember, I saw a rainbow. This wasn't just any rainbow—I saw every color, including purple. In that moment I heard God clearly say, "Here I am. I've never left you." Whether you've had the most amazing day or one of your lowest, I pray *you* hear *God say to you*, "I'm here. I've never left you." I pray this brings you peace and comfort tonight. I pray you go to bed knowing you are loved more than you can imagine by someone who died for you. I pray that you will choose to hear these words and accept that God *is* speaking to *you* tonight—not your friend or someone else—but *you*!

Out of all the things I feel God has led me to do, this is by far the one that brings me the most joy. I pray you're finding it to be an inspiration. I pray you will invite others who you think might like and benefit from it to share my journey as well.

We are braver and stronger together.

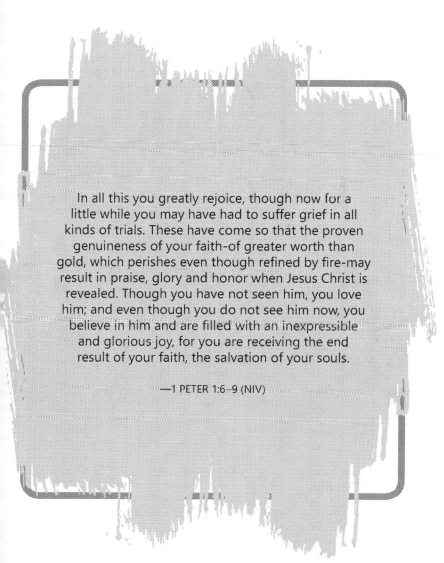

In all this you greatly rejoice, though now for a little while you may have had to suffer grief in all kinds of trials. These have come so that the proven genuineness of your faith-of greater worth than gold, which perishes even though refined by fire-may result in praise, glory and honor when Jesus Christ is revealed. Though you have not seen him, you love him; and even though you do not see him now, you believe in him and are filled with an inexpressible and glorious joy, for you are receiving the end result of your faith, the salvation of your souls.

—1 PETER 1:6–9 (NIV)

esterday James and I were talking about absolutely nothing when I suddenly said, "I've done all I can do. I've tried everything I can think of. There is *absolutely nothing* else I can do."

He said, "I understand!"

We were both having the same thoughts and feelings. Neither had any idea where to go or what to do next. It's a crazy and stressful time we are living in right now. I know God has a plan. I know God can do anything *according to His will.* We both know this. I believe this!

But the next words out of my mouth were, "*But where is He?*"

Yep, I was asking where God was. I don't see him. I don't feel him working. To be honest, that's where I am. That's how I feel. I've been saved for twenty-two years now. He told me to take up my cross and follow Him. He made promises twenty-two years ago, and I'm still waiting. I'm still searching. I'm coming out of a season where I was the closest to God I have ever been to a place where it's like my mind is blank. My heart is blank. I have no hopes, no dreams, and no idea where to go or how to make my way back to where I was.

Lost, I opened up one of my devotionals that I'd put down for a while. I needed a break. I tried to find myself, find God, find where I was, find my dreams, and find my joy, peace, and my place. The devotion I turned to should have been read three months earlier; however, I'm a firm believer that things also happen in *God's time.* That message wasn't meant for me three months ago; it had been set aside for when I needed to hear it—when I was searching for hope and searching for God. The first sentence of the second paragraph read, "He wants to challenge you to show you what He can do when you can't."

We need to open our hearts. We need to give God control so that He can do what we can't. God doesn't want or need us to do anything other than trust Him. That doesn't mean we should sit idly by doing nothing. We need to seek Him. Seek His will. Seek His plan. God is still here. He's still in control. He hasn't forgotten you. He sees your tears. He sees your pain. He sees your broken heart.

He is saying, "Trust Me." Trust His plan. Trust His timing. Trust His will.

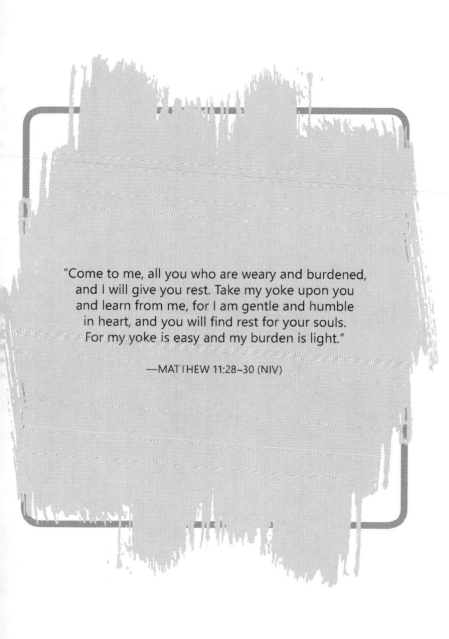

"Come to me, all you who are weary and burdened,
and I will give you rest. Take my yoke upon you
and learn from me, for I am gentle and humble
in heart, and you will find rest for your souls.
For my yoke is easy and my burden is light."

—MATTHEW 11:28–30 (NIV)

I had a friend a couple of years ago say, "But no one asked you to do that."

In that moment I heard what she said, and it clicked. But as time passed, it didn't actually sink in. I'd heard it but didn't practice it. I quickly fell right back into the same old patterns. In the middle of an ordinary day God changed my perspective on a lot of things (a story I'll continue later). I realized, I mean *actually* realized, that I had placed these expectations on myself that no one had ever asked of me.

Our circumstances had changed, and I somehow convinced myself I had to do something about it. I had to help! *But,* in this moment, I finally realized—no one had asked me to. I placed all these expectations on myself, but no one had ever actually said I needed to do all these extra things. Y'all, my heart broke in that moment because I realized it had robbed me of so much. I'd exerted all this extra time and energy into something I was never asked, much less expected, to do. Instead of enjoying moments by pausing, reflecting, and gradually continuing, I pushed myself each day to do more and more, consuming my time with things that ultimately didn't matter. Instead of taking a deep breath and soaking in the moments I was given, I inadvertently took them for granted, and now I can't have those moments again. Once a moment has passed, you can't get it back. My only hope is to one day be blessed enough to have an opportunity to make new moments. But I can't allow fear, worry, doubt, and guilt to control me.

Sometimes we are allowed to walk down paths that teach us lessons we might not have otherwise learned. Every day I remind myself that no one asked me to do this. There are moments I've fallen back into this pattern, but I'm working on progress, not perfection. Each day I'm trying to be better than the day before, but I'm not perfect. I remind myself often during the day so I don't pick up what I was asked to put down.

I don't know whether this speaks to anyone other than me, but if it does, I pray you will take this moment to breathe. You're one person who can only do so much. Give yourself some slack. No one will judge you but you. I pray that you've placed an expectation on yourself that no one actually asked you to do. Give yourself grace, and give God control!

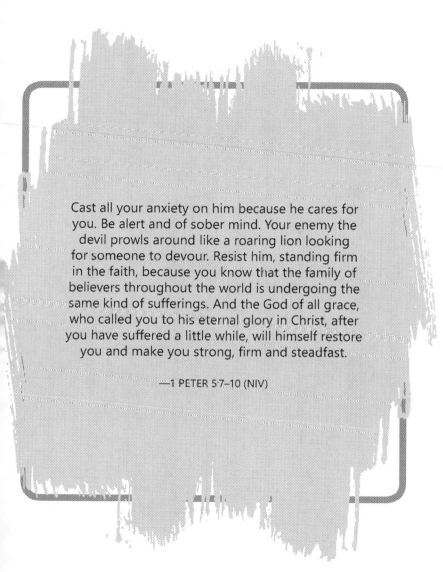

Cast all your anxiety on him because he cares for you. Be alert and of sober mind. Your enemy the devil prowls around like a roaring lion looking for someone to devour. Resist him, standing firm in the faith, because you know that the family of believers throughout the world is undergoing the same kind of sufferings. And the God of all grace, who called you to his eternal glory in Christ, after you have suffered a little while, will himself restore you and make you strong, firm and steadfast.

—1 PETER 5:7–10 (NIV)

I was happy and content with where my life was and with the direction it was going. In an instant that changed. I've spent some time trying to gather my thoughts. Trying to figure out—once again—how do I go on from here and wondering why. While I was praying about one aspect of my life, we suddenly *all* got slapped with a *huge* uncertainty. Our world was completely changed in an instant. We were living our normal, everyday lives, and then suddenly we weren't. We didn't know what each new day would bring.

The emergence of COVID-19 in 2020 had our world facing times many had never seen or even dreamed of. I know my family's lives have been shattered by this epidemic—not just from the fear of the unknown about the virus itself and living in isolation, but we were also having to educate our kids from home. Many things have kept my mind racing, but I realized how much of an impact what's going on around us has on our livelihood. Our business depended on schools, programs, weddings, businesses, and shoppers. But the world kind of shut down, and we had zero, I mean *zero*, income. If that doesn't scare a person, then I'm not sure they're human.

So we had no income, not to mention the worry that this virus could impact our parents and child. To say I was scared would be an understatement. To say I wasn't worried would be a lie. I was on the verge of having a complete meltdown as the world around us was changing by the minute, and there was absolutely *nothing* we could do. I felt completely hopeless and helpless. The reality was that businesses would fail, and people could lose everything. Lives were being lost, and it broke my heart. I *could not* sit there asking people to support my business when I was worried about how I was going to pay my own bills.

Those first few weeks of the pandemic were extremely hard on me. I couldn't begin to imagine what the next weeks and months would look like. I was scared! But I took a deep breath, listened to the complete silence of no phone ringing, and I looked out at my empty store and the empty street outside. I could feel God's peace! I didn't know how we'd make it through those next months. I didn't know how we'd pay our bills, and I certainly didn't know when we would get work again, but I did trust that God had this! God and God alone was in control.

God makes the way, even when I can't see how it will come together. It might not be exactly what I want, and it may not be in the easiest or most comfortable way, but He will provide. We just have to trust.

If you were like me and felt scared and worried during the pandemic, I hope next time life turns upside down, you can trust that God is in control. I hope you find comfort knowing you're not alone and that God loves you. He will make a way, even when there it doesn't seem possible. Take a deep breath, let go, and let God have control!

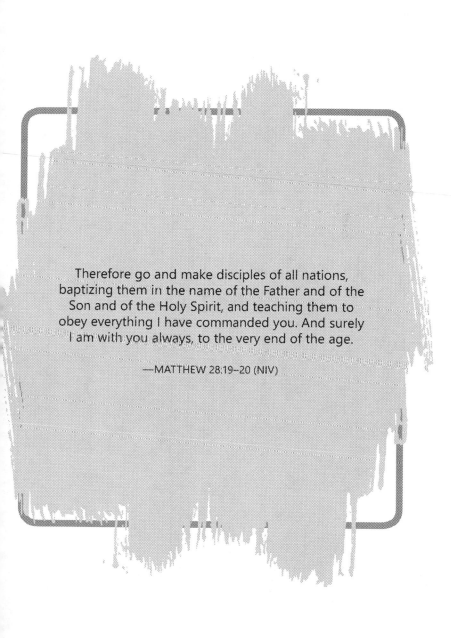

Therefore go and make disciples of all nations, baptizing them in the name of the Father and of the Son and of the Holy Spirit, and teaching them to obey everything I have commanded you. And surely I am with you always, to the very end of the age.

—MATTHEW 28:19–20 (NIV)

There are times when your heart is full of fear and doubt, and you can't make sense of all the chaos surrounding you. There are times when you feel like you're exactly where you're supposed to be, doing exactly what you're supposed to be doing, and yet nothing seems to be changing or working out. There may be times when the reality of your decreasing bank account and increasing debt starts affecting everything around you.

You may stand with tears flowing down your cheeks and your heart broken, desperately wanting to wave the white flag. You will think you've finally hit your breaking point. You're done; you can't fight anymore. You have no idea, how or why, but instead of giving up, you can decide to stand taller than you've ever stood before. You look up to the One who created you, loves you, and fights for you. Why? Because you realize the enemy is trying to crush your hope—the hope of Jesus. If you give up, the enemy wins. Instead of giving up, stand up, look the enemy in the eyes, and tell him to go back to hell because he has no authority over you or your life. You are chosen, redeemed, set apart, and loved by God. God created you for a purpose, and you are going to fight like you've never fought before.

Get up, and *fight*! Take back your life! God didn't create you to live in a hole full of fear. He created you to be a light that shines brightly in the darkness for Him. It *is not* easy, but He died on a cross so you could live. It's not about you or how easy you want your life to be. It's about *God*! It's about loving others. It's about fighting. It's about you giving someone else hope through sharing your struggles, your story. Stop complaining, and start moving. Be fearless! Allow God to set your soul on fire for what breaks *His* heart. It's all about Jesus—not you.

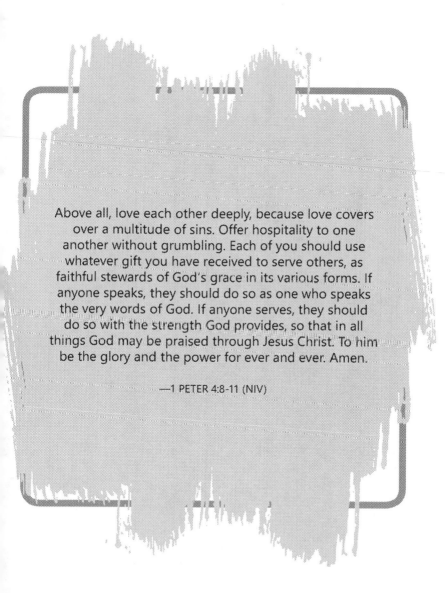

Above all, love each other deeply, because love covers over a multitude of sins. Offer hospitality to one another without grumbling. Each of you should use whatever gift you have received to serve others, as faithful stewards of God's grace in its various forms. If anyone speaks, they should do so as one who speaks the very words of God. If anyone serves, they should do so with the strength God provides, so that in all things God may be praised through Jesus Christ. To him be the glory and the power for ever and ever. Amen.

—1 PETER 4:8-11 (NIV)

Today I watched a man sit beside a little girl who was crying. The other kids all had family members surrounding their desks at school, taking photos and cheering as they got awards, but no one was there to celebrate this one girl. After the awards had been distributed, the teacher passed out a keepsake book for each child to look at with his or her family. The little girl who had no one was still very upset. She laid her head on the table and wept. A man from another child's group came over, knelt down, and opened her book for her. As he joyfully admired her creations, you could see he wanted to cheer her up just a little.

This man could have chosen to ignore her and see his own child's artwork, but instead he decided to sit and comfort a lonely little girl. I don't know how the story ends or if she eventually smiled. I don't know if he made her day or not. I do know that in this moment I realized I needed to be more like this man. I'm not sure whether anyone else noticed this interaction. Maybe some even assumed she was his child, but I knew the truth. God gives us moments in life when we can be the hands and feet of Christ, but if we don't pay attention, we can miss our opportunity to change someone's life. I pray that, though she may be small, this man's act really did bring this little girl some comfort knowing that a kind man with a little compassion took time to sit and talk with her.

Sometimes all it takes is a small act of kindness to change someone's life. It's so easy to get caught up in our own lives and problems that we miss these opportunities. Are you willing to open your heart today? Are you willing to be the hands and feet of Jesus for someone today?

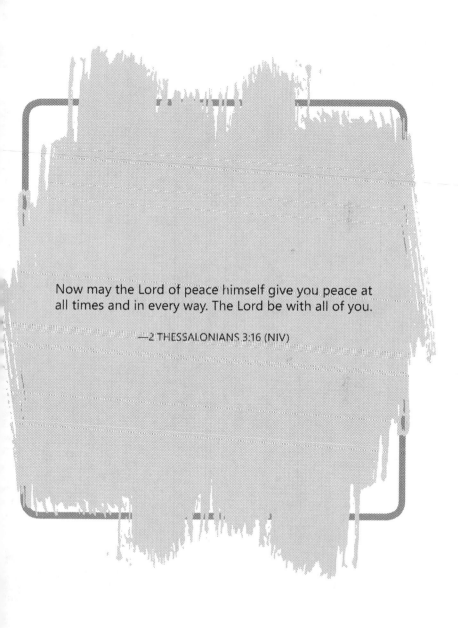

Now may the Lord of peace himself give you peace at all times and in every way. The Lord be with all of you.

—2 THESSALONIANS 3:16 (NIV)

The peace that comes from God is the single greatest feeling in the world. Why try to control your life, your family, your finances, your hopes and dreams, your job, or—better yet—anything at all? When you can let go of control, you can let go of your past, your expectations, your regrets, and your hopes.

When we allow ourselves to truly let go, unspeakable peace and joy flood our souls. Even better than having these amazing feelings is sharing them with others. We are not just happy, but full of joy that now our kids see and feel. Our spouses get to experience a new, more powerful, confident, amazing person who can help show them a better way. Let go! Take a deep breath, and allow everything to go as you exhale the weight of the world you've carried way too long. It can now be carried by the only One who can take it all.

I'm telling you I've experienced this peace and joy and it's an indescribable feeling. It *can* heal the deepest wounds and shine light on the darkest places. I pray everyone experiences this. Lives are saved and forever changed by this peace and joy. Help save a life. You may never know how one smile, one hello, one helping hand, a "how are you today," one handshake, one free meal, one gift, one letter, one ego check can forever change the life of its recipient. There are people all over the world who are waiting for you to show them hope and love and how they can find peace.

Will you answer the call, or will you crawl back into your safe space with bitterness and anger, blaming everyone but yourself for not doing anything? We don't all have to believe the same things or dare to point fingers, but we can all make changes in the lives of those around us. After all, God created us for a purpose far greater than ourselves.

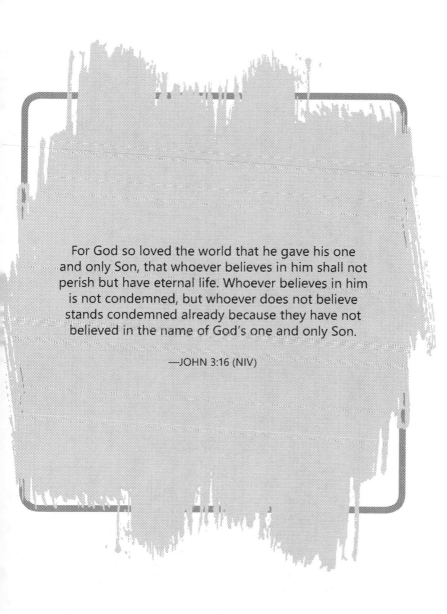

For God so loved the world that he gave his one
and only Son, that whoever believes in him shall not
perish but have eternal life. Whoever believes in him
is not condemned, but whoever does not believe
stands condemned already because they have not
believed in the name of God's one and only Son.

—JOHN 3:16 (NIV)

*A*s I sat at the table last night with Chloe, waiting for James and Burke to get home, I stared out our kitchen window. The barren early-winter trees blew back and forth, and I watched them sway with each gust of wind. The sky was overcast, and the entire atmosphere exuded a chill. I noticed a small ray of light filtering down between two trees. Everything else looked dreary, but that one sunbeam stood out in contrast. Chloe noticed me staring and turned to see what I was looking at; however, it would be impossible to catch it without *really* looking.

I read something today that reminded me of a moment when I sat out on our front porch, marveling at all God had done. As I sat there, I searched my soul, trying to locate what I was holding onto and not letting go. What was I keeping from God? In that instant, I realized that everything I had ever wanted and then gotten hadn't turned out like I'd expected it to. Sitting out on our porch, staring into the sky, I let go of it all—all my plans, ideas, and dreams—because I realized they will never be as good as what God has planned.

I realized God was reminding me that He is still God. He is still good. He is still in control. Everything around us may be falling apart or not working out like we want, but if we keep our eyes on Him, He will not fail. A ray of light gives hope in the midst of uncertainty. Sometimes a ray of light is all you need. I don't know what lies ahead on the road for us. I'm tired of waiting, wondering, and questioning, but I'm also tired of my dreams that don't fulfill our purpose. Wait, hope, and pray, and most of all, we should seek God. His plans are so much better than anything we could ever dream.

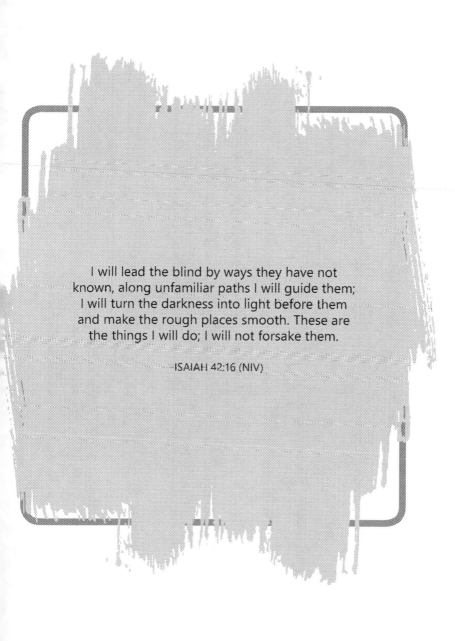

I will lead the blind by ways they have not
known, along unfamiliar paths I will guide them;
I will turn the darkness into light before them
and make the rough places smooth. These are
the things I will do; I will not forsake them.

—ISAIAH 42:16 (NIV)

We were heading to get dessert after finishing dinner at our favorite restaurant when I stopped and looked at my husband. My heart smiled. My heart was full of joy and happiness—not because everything was perfect or because I had the perfect marriage, the perfect children, the perfect body, or the perfect job—but because I had the perfect God.

In a matter of thirty seconds, I processed where I'd been one year before versus where I was in that moment. We'd gone from the ER to owning a business, to multiple doctor visits for allergy testing for Burke and me, Burke's four ear infections, celebrating nineteen years together and our twelfth wedding anniversary, our first trip away from the kids, Chloe's broken arm, some very difficult situations, watching our little boy graduate preschool, our baby girl being potty-trained and heading into preschool, making memories at the pool and the beach and everywhere in between, and then venturing out into direct sales with impressive accomplishments. We had gone from having a bright future, full of passion, love, and hope to falling into a bottomless pit with no hope or idea how to continue, keep fighting, or find what was lost.

When I looked at James and heard my kids being completely silly and ridiculous behind us, my soul smiled. Even through all the tears, hurt, joy, and happiness I am already blessed every day that I get to spend time with them. God continues to bless me when I deserve nothing. I often forget to thank Him, talk with Him, or even just remember Him, and yet He blesses me still.

I don't know what to do right now. I don't know where I'm going or how I'm getting there. I don't know how I'm going to pay bills or have time to invest in everything that needs my attention. What I do know is that I'm going to disappoint God the most and my family, friends, customers, and self a lot. I'm going to struggle with where I'm at and why nothing ever works out or changes. I'm going to take one step forward and twenty steps back, but I'm not staying there.

Sometimes it will be easy, sometimes it will be harder, but I *refuse* to give up. My life hasn't been for nothing. Every laugh, smile, tear, pain, struggle, victory, and blessing has been for a greater purpose—His purpose. So no matter how bright or dark everything looks through our lenses, I pray you will find something or someone to thank God for. I pray that, even through the tears and pain and even though you might be hurting and questioning, you know you're not alone. I pray you know you are loved by Someone who thought you were worth dying for. I pray that God will give you peace and comfort or whatever it is that you need tonight.

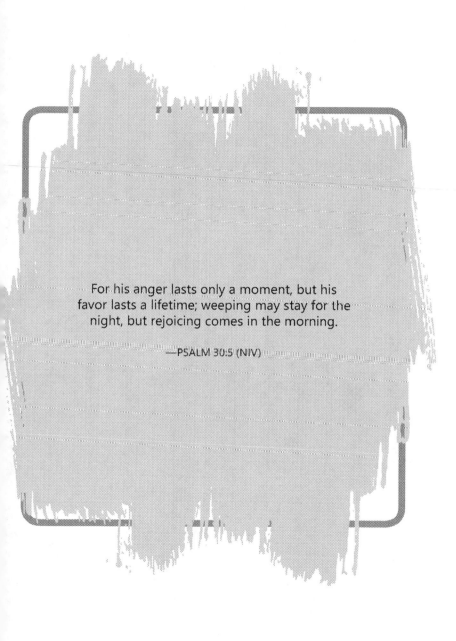

For his anger lasts only a moment, but his favor lasts a lifetime; weeping may stay for the night, but rejoicing comes in the morning.

—PSALM 30:5 (NIV)

hat do I do now? God, I don't want to go in.
God, I truly don't want to go in. Inside, my mind becomes foggy and filled with doubt, loneliness, and heavy weights that seem too heavy to bear. Once I didn't want to leave this place and couldn't wait to get back to it. Now it's become such a burden and a huge weight to carry every day. A place I loved became a place I despise with every fiber of my being. I want to be set free from the prison where this place keeps my mind and my spirit.

It feels like I'm chained in my mind. I'm fighting to break free, but freedom doesn't come—just more heaviness in my mind and soul. Dreams seem to be coming true for those around me, and it's so incredibly hard to keep moving, believing, and having faith when I'm drained hourly in this prison, fighting to just keep going. I want my life back. I want my mind back. I want to be set free. I want to escape this prison that has me struggling to believe everything I know is real.

I just don't want to go in. I know what awaits me inside, and I just don't want to do this anymore. Rescue me from this place, and set me free from this prison. Our minds can seem like prisons that we can't escape sometimes. I pray when you find yourself in this prison you will cry out to God. Ask him to come in this moment with you. When you need help, never be afraid to ask for it. There is no shame in seeking help beyond our abilities.

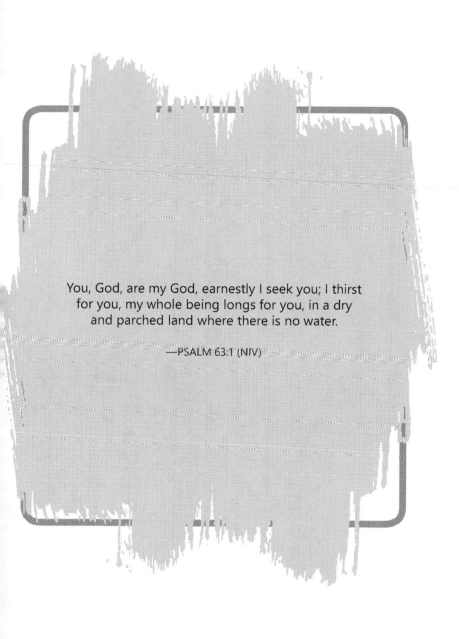

You, God, are my God, earnestly I seek you; I thirst for you, my whole being longs for you, in a dry and parched land where there is no water.

—PSALM 63:1 (NIV)

I—*came looking for You today, but I didn't find You. I only have memories of where I've found You before. I wanted You to show up. I wanted You to be there in that moment. I wanted You to quiet the questions in my mind. Where are You? I've given You all I have. I'm here waiting.*

So often we want God to show up the moment we whisper His name—the very moment we feel desperate for Him—the moment *we* want Him too. But do we ever stop to think that God's already there? He actually never left. If you've been wondering where God is in the middle of your pain, your suffering, your shame, and your loss, he's been beside you the whole time.

Take a deep breath, and look around—not with your eyes, but with your heart. Do you feel that small peace that tells you, no matter what's going on, it's going to be OK? You don't know how or why, but deep down you can feel it is so. That's God! He was there then, and He's still here now. You just have to trust. It's called faith. Sometimes you just have to trust. If you knew and felt God every time, then how would your faith grow? Faith isn't seeing God. Faith is believing that, even though you can't see Him, He's still there.

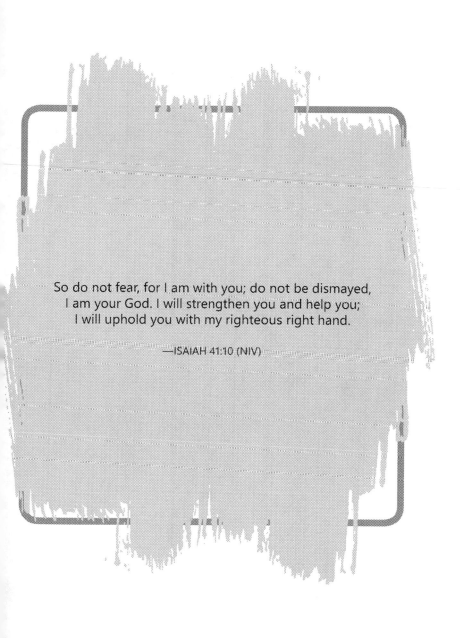

So do not fear, for I am with you; do not be dismayed,
I am your God. I will strengthen you and help you;
I will uphold you with my righteous right hand.

—ISAIAH 41:10 (NIV)

*O*n February 28, 2011, I was sobbing hysterically on our living room floor. My husband was out playing basketball with friends. I tried calling some close friends, but they hadn't answered their phones. I had no idea why I was even crying, but I knew I was scared.

You see, that was the day I found out I was pregnant with our son, Burke. To understand the story, you have to know that we never planned to have children. It was a topic that was often brought up—especially since we'd been married for six years at that time.

I never wanted my kids to live in a world in which they didn't get to experience my dad. I often had long talks about that with God.

For the first eight or nine weeks of my pregnancy, I was terrified that James would divorce me.

At our first appointment, there wasn't a heartbeat. I'd been lying in bed the night before and had felt something inside my stomach I'd never felt before. It was almost like butterflies. The next morning when I woke up, the fluttering pattern wasn't there, and I knew instinctively what that meant. However, I also knew that I'd caught it early.

When the sonographer looked all around my belly during my ultrasound and couldn't locate my baby, I was scared. There could have been so many feelings in the moment, but she said she was sure it was just too early to see anything. We could come back in a week or two to recheck.

The next week we came back, and sure enough, she found his heartbeat.

We didn't get to have lunch together often because James worked in a neighboring city, which made that day perfect for having lunch together at McAlister's.

Y'all, I was still terrified. He had no idea I was on the edge of losing it. We began to talk about what the pregnancy meant. We discussed how and when we'd tell our families and friends, and we decided to just be thankful in that moment.

We'd never planned to be where we were, but we knew what a miracle we'd been blessed with. You see, we discovered we'd both been praying the same prayer. God's will happens in God's time. If we were meant to have a child, God would make the way when the time was right.

I realized James wasn't going to leave me. He was excited. He definitely accepted it from day one. I, on the other hand, was nervous the whole time.

Each morning I woke up with a grateful heart, knowing I could be like so many who'd lost this very blessing. I've had a hard time my whole life believing good things were meant for me. I so desperately wanted this little boy growing inside me to be OK. It wasn't until he came into the world I truly accepted the gift God meant for us to have.

We dedicated both of our kids to God. The verse we used for each was so fitting. It might have been the same, but each of our children have different stories about who they are, how they came to be, and who they will become one day.

First Samuel 1:27 says, "I prayed for this child, and the Lord has granted me what I asked of him."

Never be too scared to talk to someone. Never be too scared to share your story. Never be too scared to be real with someone. God knew what we needed long before we ever did. I didn't know everything was going to be OK. All I knew was that I trusted God had a plan. I didn't know what it was, but I knew it was going to be OK.

Sometimes we don't know how it's going to be OK. Sometimes we don't believe it's going to be OK. Sometimes we have to just let go and trust that it is and will be. God knows your story. God knows the plans He has for you. Will you trust Him today?

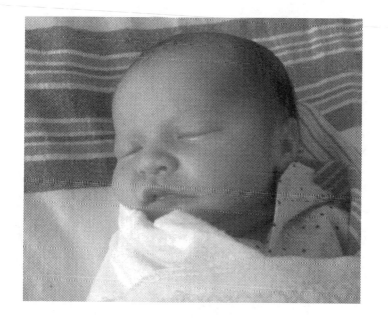

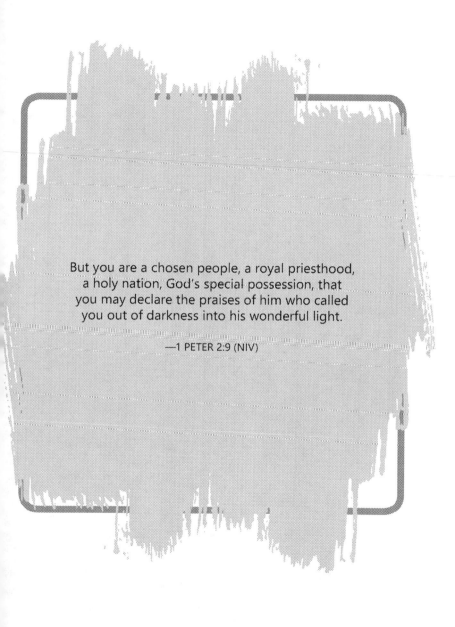

But you are a chosen people, a royal priesthood,
a holy nation, God's special possession, that
you may declare the praises of him who called
you out of darkness into his wonderful light.

—1 PETER 2:9 (NIV)

S taying in your comfort zone will get you *nowhere* close to where you want to be. We all have little bubbles that we love to live in, but the Bible doesn't ask us to stay inside those warm, cozy shelters. Jesus didn't die on a cross and rise on the third day so that we could just stay comfortable. We were created for something far greater than our little safe zones.

There was a message our pastor preached once that has stuck with me for a very long time. I try to remind myself of it all the time—especially when things are difficult. The message had to do with living out the life Jesus called us to. In this message the pastor said, "If it were easy, everyone would do it."

I knew in that moment I didn't want to be like everyone else. I know this thought pattern has gotten me in a lot of trouble over the years, but in the end, I don't want to look back and see that I gave up. It's easy to give up. It's easy to not care. I want to look back and see that I kept fighting, even when I was fighting from my knees.

I so desperately want you to experience the freedom that can only come from God. When you finally decide that today you're going to stop being scared and get outside your comfort zone for God, you'll do it. God didn't send His only Son into this world to die a death He didn't deserve to save our souls for us to just give up and take the easy road. He didn't die for us to stop fighting or to stay in our little bubbles. He died so we could live.

I hope this inspires you to do more for God and get out of your comfort zone a little. I pray this lights a fire inside you. Each of us has our own stories, inspirations, and experiences that could help save a life. Don't allow the fear of judgment from others to keep you from sharing your story. Everyone has skeletons; they're just hiding in different closets.

Your story could save a life.

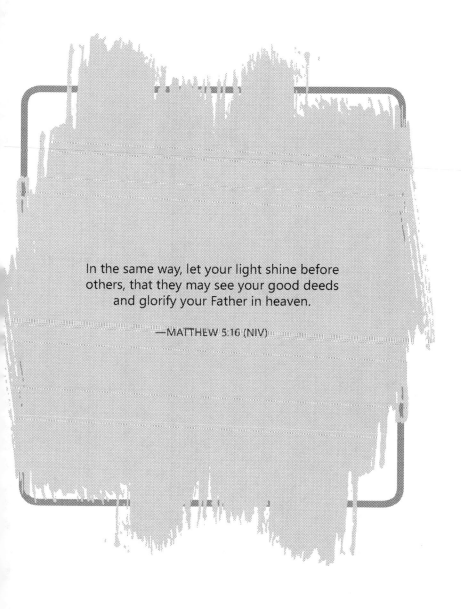

In the same way, let your light shine before others, that they may see your good deeds and glorify your Father in heaven.

—MATTHEW 5:16 (NIV)

There was a moment when I realized I wanted to do more. I've tried so many things over the years, thinking each was what God wanted me to do or what he'd led me to do. So I created a group in which I felt I could share. Actually a lot of what's in this book was taken from realizations I had in that group.

I had this vision that I'd do a live video in this group the day before I originally wrote the post in that group. I think I announced I would do it the next day so people had the chance to plan to watch if they wanted. I remember being so excited, not only about this group, but about doing this live video. It was nothing fancy, just talking a little bit about who I was and why I'd decided to create the group.

Honest confession: *I woke up excited that morning, but y'all, the nerves kicked in.*

I added a few people the day before going live that I loved to follow, and all the things I don't like about myself—my fear of talking to people, my self-esteem issues—all wore on me so bad that I chickened out.

That day, I allowed negative thoughts about myself and what I thought I couldn't do to rule.

Why? Out of fear!

In that moment I was so terrified of what that group would think of me. I'm not the best speaker. I'm not the most popular person. In that moment, I thought I had nothing to offer anyone. I had this preconceived notion of who I was compared to the person God saw in me.

We are all growing and learning. Some days we'll feel like we failed, but those are the days when we'll grow more than we realize.

There will be days when we allow fear to overcome us, and that's OK. Just don't allow yourself to stay in the fear.

I tell people all the time that when they make fun of me for being a scaredy-cat, they're not hurting my feelings at all. I will own it!

I got chicken today, and I'm OK with that.

I pray that in the moments when you find yourself fearful instead of fearless, you will pause and give yourself a break. It's OK! God sees you. He knows you. He's ready to help. All you have to do is ask.

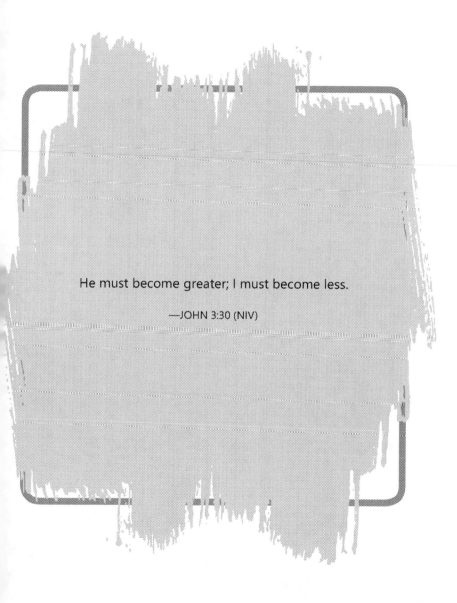

He must become greater; I must become less.

—JOHN 3:30 (NIV)

In 2018 God opened the door for me to leave my full-time job. This meant huge changes for our family. Deciding to leave my job meant our daughter could no longer attend the daycare where she'd gone for most of her life. It meant she no longer got to spend time with her friends every day.

When you're only four, you can't understand what's happening. You only know that your world has changed completely. I felt so incredibly guilty for making that decision. I knew it was the right one and what was best for our family, but I still cried just about every day, knowing this was my fault. At that time I couldn't see the good. I couldn't see the plan in the making. I could only see that my daughter was sad and felt it was my fault.

It was a difficult year, being away from her friends and the routine she'd known since she was six months old. We shed a lot of tears, but we've also laughed and have spent a lot of irreplaceable time together.

She was a little apprehensive about starting "big-girl" school, yet managed to do extremely well. She quickly adapted and was having great days at school.

But today this little girl has a smile so big there's no denying God's goodness. I wanted to pray so many times for Him to work this out the way I wanted, and I'd cried so many nights because it hadn't.

I didn't want it to be about what she wanted or what I wanted for her, but about what God's plan was for her. His path that He wanted for her was what was important—not mine.

As moms, we do our best to make things possible, but we usually can't. However, it is without a doubt that God created a way when there was no way. God opened the doors and closed the doors that needed opening and closing.

God, thank you so incredibly much for your faithfulness and goodness to us, even when we don't deserve it and can't see it.

That night our little girl went to sleep full of joy, because her best friend was now attending her school and was in her class.

God can fix things unexpectedly in your situation too. God can move and open the doors that you can't see.

When I made the decision that forever changed our lives, I couldn't see through the guilt. It's not through our sight that we can see God working and moving. Sometimes we just have to be patient and let God work.

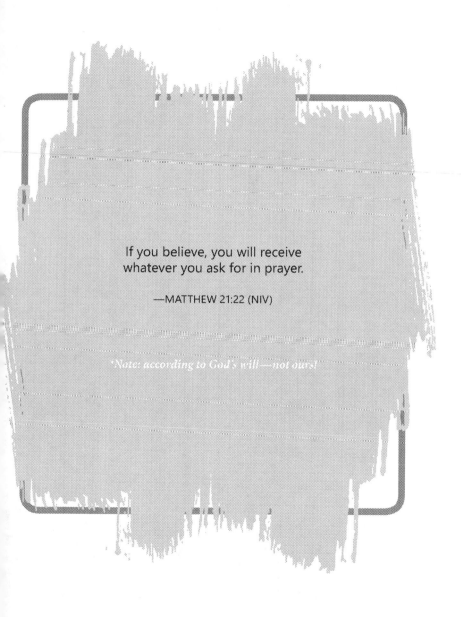

If you believe, you will receive
whatever you ask for in prayer.

—MATTHEW 21:22 (NIV)

Note: according to God's will—not ours!

I will never forget the day I told my best friend that God had the perfect girl for him. I told him that one day God would send a girl into his life who would love him just as much as he loved her.

I didn't know who God would send him.

I didn't know when God would send her.

I just knew that in that moment, when he was doubting God and what God said, I wanted him to know God did hear him. God would answer his prayers. I wanted him to keep believing, even when he wanted to give up.

Sometimes in life you just need someone to remind you that God is here. God hears you. God has a plan. Just keep believing.

Boy, was I shocked. I never in a million years could have imagined *that girl* would turn out to be me. He could've chosen anyone, but he chose me. He could've loved anyone, but he loves me still. Seventeen years ago he could've married anyone, but he married me.

I will never understand why, but I will spend my life thanking God for answering my prayer. I prayed God would send a man who would love me for me. I wanted a man who loved me, but loved God even more. I needed a man who would not only accept my struggles, but would strive to help support me when I can't support myself.

I prayed for a man who would hold me and wipe the tears from my eyes and who would love me, even when I don't love myself. I wanted a man who would believe in me, even when I didn't believe in myself and who would hurt when I hurt, laugh when I laugh, and cry when I cry.

My husband will never fully understand how incredible he is.

My actions don't always represent the love, appreciation, and thankfulness my heart feels for him. The last seventeen years have rarely been easy, but we continue to fight for our marriage. We continue to seek God more, not only in the difficult times, but in the good times too.

We are not perfect. Our marriage isn't perfect. Our lives aren't perfect. But as long as we continue to seek the One who is perfect first, we will continue to make each other smile like no one else can. We will continue to love each other like no one else can.

God didn't say it was going to be easy. He said it would be *worth it*. I'm excited to see where God continues to lead as we follow Him.

Jesus died a death He didn't deserve so we could live. *He* has continued to bless me, though I deserve nothing. *He* loves me, though I often fail Him. After all I've done, *He* sent a man into my life who I continue to frustrate to no end, yet he loves me unconditionally.

He not only sent this man to love me, but He reminds me that I am loved more than I will ever know, not only by my husband and our kids, but by God.

Lord, there are no words with which I can properly express my gratitude. I pray that we continue to seek You, Your will, and Your way above all else. I pray You will give strength to those who need strength to keep fighting. I pray You give hope to the hopeless. I pray You move mountains for those who need to know You are the Creator of heaven and earth and that You haven't forgotten them. I pray they know You are working in and through their lives, even though they can't see it.

We haven't had a fairy-tale marriage. It has rarely been easy. We've done plenty of fighting. We've had a lot of tears and anger. We didn't make it this far by giving up. We didn't make it this far by allowing the devil to win. We didn't make it this far by ourselves.

My hope and prayer have always been that our marriage, our struggles, and our lives could be used to help someone else. If I could narrow it down to one thing that helped me keep fighting and keep going, it's that I stopped looking to my husband to fulfill me and looked to God instead.

There is a song by Sanctus Real called "Lead Me." When times were hard, I'd sing this song, desperately wanting my husband to be and do what this song says.

One day, as I stood at our dishwasher, tears pouring down my cheeks, I realized I didn't need my husband to be and do those things in the song. I needed my God to be and do those things.

From that moment, things started to change. I changed my perspective on who needed to change, and it wasn't my husband. I needed to look within me. Our issues weren't all his fault, and they weren't going to magically fix themselves. Expecting my husband to change without first looking at my own heart could never solve any problems.

If we're truly honest with ourselves, we'll see we aren't perfect either. When you feel like your marriage is struggling, I pray you will cling to God harder and more strongly than you ever have.

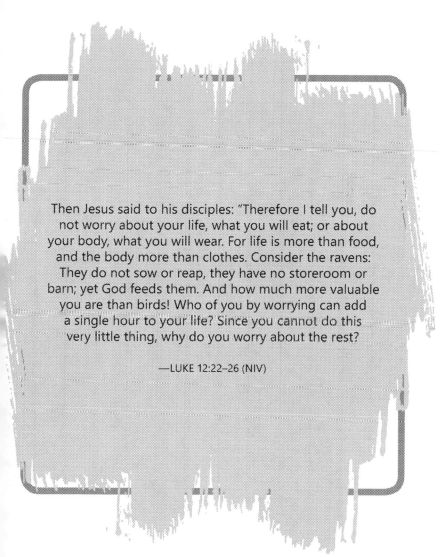

Then Jesus said to his disciples: "Therefore I tell you, do not worry about your life, what you will eat; or about your body, what you will wear. For life is more than food, and the body more than clothes. Consider the ravens: They do not sow or reap, they have no storeroom or barn; yet God feeds them. And how much more valuable you are than birds! Who of you by worrying can add a single hour to your life? Since you cannot do this very little thing, why do you worry about the rest?

—LUKE 12:22–26 (NIV)

S ome experiences stick with you, even when you don't want them too.

I'd been in labor all day with my son when the doctor became concerned I was getting an infection and decided I needed to have a C-section. Despite the area being numbed, I could feel the pain from the knife the whole time.

At the moment we discovered we were having our daughter, I'd asked our doctor if we could schedule a C-section for her birth, and the day finally arrived for us to meet our little girl.

My first C-section hadn't been planned, so I'd had no idea what to expect. I was just praying the medicine would work this time so I wouldn't feel the same pain I had before.

If you've ever had a C-section, you'll know they say, "This is the only thing we will ask you to do today," as you lift yourself off one bed and onto the other in your room.

As I did this, my husband took our then three-year-old son with him to go pick up his parents. My mom stepped out of the room to give me some privacy as well.

I lifted my bottom, and as I went to move to the other bed, I started to hemorrhage. The nurses frantically started working to try and control the bleeding.

In that moment I had no idea what was happening. I only knew I was getting super-hot and sweaty and didn't feel good. I heard what the nurses were saying, but I was terrified and numb.

My mom stood outside the door helplessly as she watched all these nurses rushing to my room. I heard them keep asking whether they should call the doctor.

I kept thinking about how my husband and son had left and how everything had been fine, but in that split second, I was no longer OK. The medical staff had no idea what was happening, as I tried hard not think about how close I was to not being there.

The doctor came back and eventually got my bleeding under

control. The nurses were absolutely amazing. They made sure to comfort me, even when things got tense. I could see they were concerned and working hard to do everything in their power to help me.

I had no idea how bad it had actually been until the next day when one of my nurses stopped by to see me, wanting to make sure I was doing OK.

She said, "You scared us," and it wasn't until that moment that I fully understood how badly things could have gone.

I can't ever fully explain how that moment impacted my life. It would be an understatement to say I was scared. The memory of that day has haunted me for so long. When they finally got my bleeding under control, it didn't actually ever fully stop. It was a constant battle of, not only bleeding, but knowing that at any moment it could happen again.

I was so scared to do anything because I was terrified I was going to bleed out. This fear haunted me daily for years and kept reminding me that my family had walked out of the room and didn't even know I'd been struggling to live. To be perfectly honest, I still have days when I get scared thinking about that day. It's been seven years, but there are times when I feel the exact way I felt in that moment.

Sometimes you'll have life experiences that may take you a long time to get over or that truly never go away. Sometimes you'll have to learn to live with them. Sometimes you'll have to keep moving forward, even in fear. It's OK.

I pray when these memories come back that you don't live in them like I did. Remember to be thankful you made it through. He was in control then, and He's still in control now. You process the effects, but you move on. Don't allow fear to grip your life.

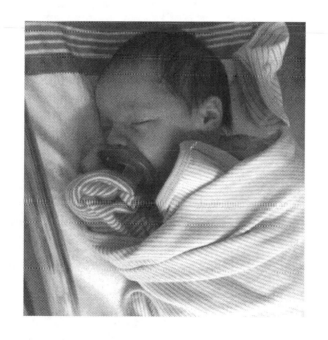

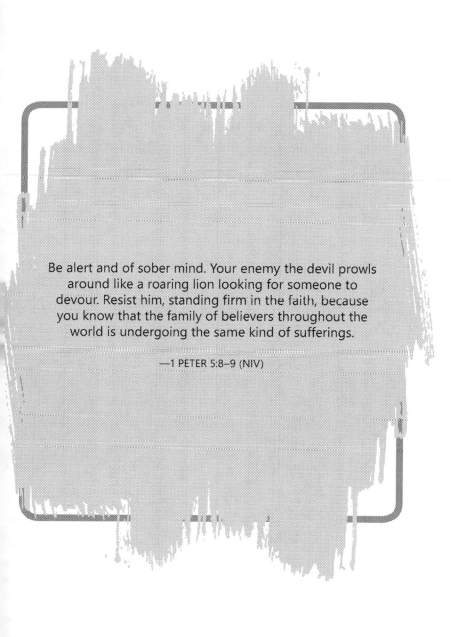

Be alert and of sober mind. Your enemy the devil prowls around like a roaring lion looking for someone to devour. Resist him, standing firm in the faith, because you know that the family of believers throughout the world is undergoing the same kind of sufferings.

—1 PETER 5:8–9 (NIV)

I n 2016 I decided to step outside my comfort zone to volunteer for a nonprofit organization called TRAC (Teen Reach Adventure Camp). TRAC focuses on abused, neglected, and at-risk teens in the foster care system. It was a three-day biblically based program.

As you step outside your comfort zone for God, the devil will try to attack you harder. When he can't reach you, he goes after your marriage, your family, or anything else he thinks he can. If he can get you to doubt, to question, to give up, or to surrender during hard times, he thinks he's won. If he can get you to not step out for God, then maybe you will give up.

Just imagine what could happen if you *didn't* give up. Imagine what could happen if you fought to do the thing God was calling you to. Imagine the joy and peace you could find. The devil knows that if you can taste the goodness of God, you'll keep wanting it.

Anytime you're stepping out and doing something that's good for God, the devil will attack you and those you love. He knows if he can keep you down, you won't be in a state to make a difference for God. But he also knows that if you fight, God will win.

God's already won! All you have to do is fight through the hard times and the attacks to realize it could be the devil trying to keep you from your destiny. This thing God is calling you to do could make a difference in someone else's life, but it could also make a difference in your own too.

Remember that the devil *wants* you to fail, so he will try everything to get that to happen. We have to stop in the hard moments and ask, *Is this just the devil trying to attack me?* It may be, but sometimes we give credit where credit isn't due. Whatever our current circumstances, they are likely due to choices we've made.

One of the greatest revelations I've had in my marriage was learning who the enemy was during a time when I was drawing closer to God. I realized the devil was trying to mess up my marriage and attack my children's health. Leaving one area of my life wouldn't work to try to attack another. It didn't make knowing better, and it definitely didn't stop the attacks, but it did help me to change my approach and my perspective in those moments. It's hard to imagine that this is possible, but friend, I'm here to say that if I can do this, you can too.

News flash! In the end, God wins! So hang on, and keep going. Keep fighting. God created you for a greater purpose than what you are feeling and doing in this moment. He's here waiting to meet you.

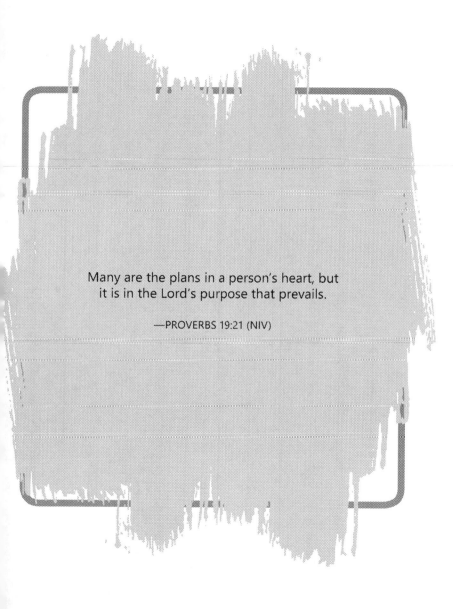

Many are the plans in a person's heart, but it is in the Lord's purpose that prevails.

—PROVERBS 19:21 (NIV)

I wish I had a magic answer to give you when you're waiting on God. It seems like all we do these days is wait. We wait on the right doors to open—wait for something to change in our lives. We wait for this chapter to be over before starting a new one.

You get up every day knowing God could change things in an instant, but He doesn't. It's another day of trying to do more than just go through the motions. Here you sit, trying to decide whether you're waiting on God or God's waiting on you. You're wondering whether you made the wrong turn or if the turn is up ahead. How far up ahead is it?

So how do you wait? How do you decide whether you're waiting on God or God's waiting on you? I'm still learning myself. So how do we wait? Here's what I've learned in my season of waiting: ask, seek, knock. These things are done together, but it's not something you do when expecting an answer. God doesn't work that way. He wants to draw you closer to Him in order to develop a relationship with you. It happens over time, not usually in an instant.

The word *ask*, in this context, is asking God to open the doors that lead to where he wants you to go. It's not a one-time question; it's continuous until the door opens or closes. We teach our kids to ask for something once, accept the answer given, and don't ask again. This isn't that kind of asking.

You must pray and ask God to open the doors *He* wants for you. You can't ask God to do this or that for you. Asking God for direction leads you to seek Him. Seek to find Him. Seek His will, His plan, and His path. When opportunities come along, test to see if they align with where you feel God is leading you in this season.

When you knock on the doors of heaven, you knock with the expectation and belief that God will answer. When you don't feel like He's there and you're just left at the door waiting, it's not because He didn't hear you or because He doesn't love you. Sometimes there are lessons during the waiting that He wants you to learn. Sometimes He tries to give you time to prepare for where He's sending you.

My friend, I don't have the answer you want to hear in your season of waiting. I can just tell you what I'm trying to do in my own season. *Ask Him.* Tell him what's on your heart. He already knows, so why not be honest? Seek Him with the intention that you won't give up until you find Him.

Knock knowing that your Father in heaven hears you and is waiting to answer the door. Just know that it might not open until after a season of waiting.

My hope and prayer is that when you find yourself waiting, you don't give up or rush into something without seeking God first.

Waiting on God may take a little longer, but in the end, His plans are so much better than our dreams. Are you seeking God for His will or for your desires?

There's nothing wrong with having dreams. I dream a lot. I have big dreams! But never let your dreams and desires overshadow God's will for your life.

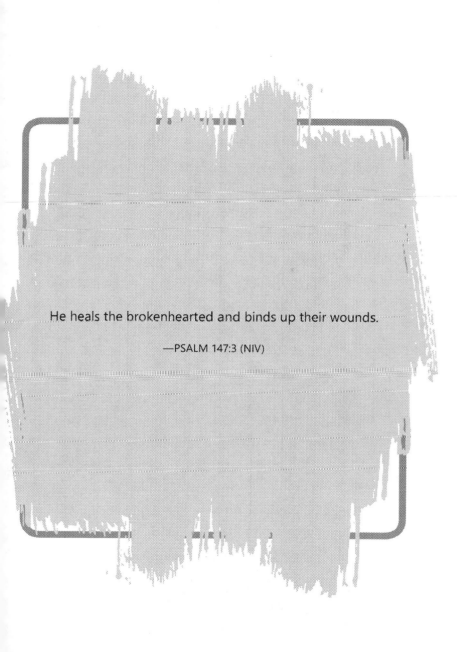

He heals the brokenhearted and binds up their wounds.

—PSALM 147:3 (NIV)

H ave you ever made a decision, only to immediately regret it? The decision couldn't be undone, so now you had to live with that choice. You may have found yourself feeling guilty and ashamed—almost dirty.

I can't describe exactly how I felt at that moment. I laid beside our dog's crate crying hysterically while my husband slept. He had no idea that I was fighting the voice in my head that said I was a killer and that it was my fault our dog who'd been sick was now dead. She wasn't sleeping in her bed like she should've been.

I found enough strength to go to my husband because I knew this darkness was a moment I couldn't fight on my own. I knew our dog wasn't eating or drinking. I knew she was suffering and that this was the best decision for her, but in this moment I felt like it was my fault. I was a killer. I'd killed our dog, and I couldn't bring her back. I should've fought for her. I shouldn't have told the doctor it was time for her to be at peace.

He'd held me and assured me it was best for her. She wasn't hurting or suffering anymore, but I just couldn't get past this moment. This decision was all my fault. Everywhere I looked I saw her. I laid in her bed and just cried.

Sometimes we have to make very difficult decisions, and the devil wants to get in our heads and try to trick us into believing we are someone or something we are not. We won't always get life right. We will make good and bad decisions and decisions that aren't easy, but we have to remember that it's not our fault.

When the darkness, shame, and guilt that come with hard decisions try to get a grip on your life, remember you are strong enough to fight the thoughts. Remember it's OK to ask for and seek help. Reach out to someone who can help you fight the darkness in that moment.

God was with me in the moment our dog went to sleep, and God was with me as I lay beside her cage crying hysterically. He was with me while my kids watched me cry in her bed. It's OK to be broken in these moments. It's OK to cry and ask God why.

I didn't know "why" that morning. I don't know why. I couldn't see it. I couldn't explain it to my kids, so we used that moment to talk about God. I told them sometimes God's will doesn't align with what we want God to do. Even though it seemed as though God wasn't answering their prayers, it didn't mean He didn't hear them or love them.

Sometimes you can't explain why things did or didn't happen in any given situation. In all the praying and trying to come to terms with the decisions we'll be faced with, I prayed for an opportunity to talk about God and this very subject of prayers not working out like we hoped. Little did I know what was going to happen. The kids desperately wanted our dog to come home and wanted to see her get better. My daughter had no idea that while she prayed for God to make Mali better, I was praying too.

At the end of a very long, heartbreaking day, I opened my heart to my daughter. I told her that sometimes she may pray and have it feel like God didn't hear her. She may pray and feel that God didn't answer her prayer the way she wanted Him too, but that didn't mean that He didn't love or hear her. I told her about my prayer and showed her that God did hear them because Mali is better because she's no longer suffering. She's just not here with us. I shared how I had prayed for a moment just like we were in, and in that moment, I realized sometimes we can't see why things happen. God still has a purpose.

Rest in peace, Mali Moo. We love and miss you.

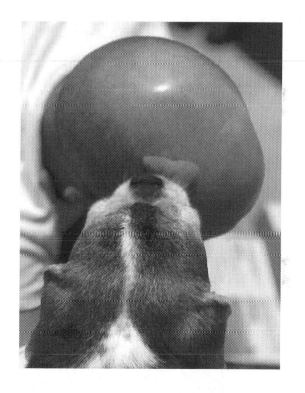

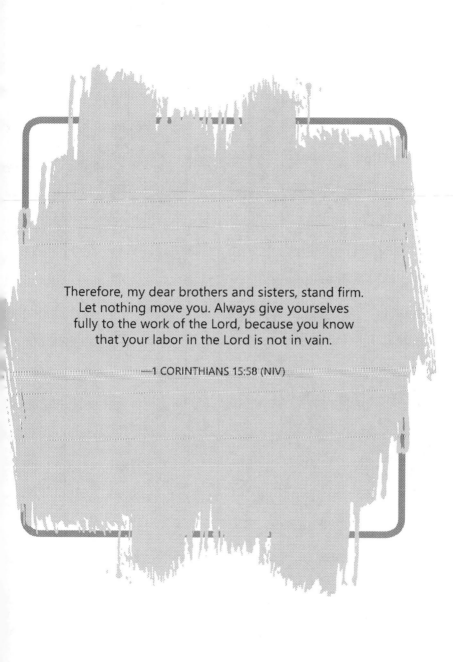

Therefore, my dear brothers and sisters, stand firm.
Let nothing move you. Always give yourselves
fully to the work of the Lord, because you know
that your labor in the Lord is not in vain.

—1 CORINTHIANS 15:58 (NIV)

*S*ometimes life feels like it's falling back into place. So you slowly take a deep breath, and the moment you go to exhale, the world seems to crash again. Instead of feeling peace and comfort; you feel heartbroken and afraid. You find yourself feeling alone and wondering what happened. What did you do? How will you ever make it this time? Why me? Why again?

Just when you finally thought nothing else could go wrong, something did. It's so hard to have faith when you can't see past the darkness. It's hard to breathe. It's hard to hold it all together. It's hard to believe. It's hard to see past the tears. In hard times it's so easy to forget God's goodness and blessings.

I've been down this road way too many times. I've seen rock bottom. I've experienced times where there seemed to be no hope. I had nothing left to fight for and no energy to fight with. The only thing holding me up were my two legs. It's a lonely place. It's OK to have questions. It's OK to wonder. It's OK to not be OK.

I can't promise everything will be OK; however, I can promise that you are never alone. When life seems impossible, hang on. Hang on for one more day. Hang on for one more breath. Be at peace that it's not about what *you* can do or how *you* can fix this, but about what *God* can and *will* do. It's not easy and may not be what you wanted, but hang on. God really does have a plan. He has a good and perfect will for you. It will be OK! You will be OK.

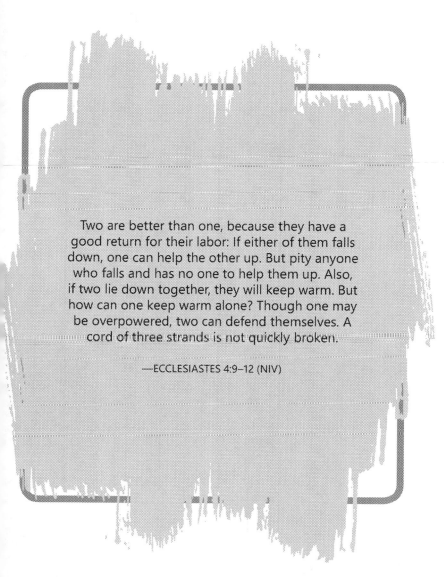

Two are better than one, because they have a good return for their labor: If either of them falls down, one can help the other up. But pity anyone who falls and has no one to help them up. Also, if two lie down together, they will keep warm. But how can one keep warm alone? Though one may be overpowered, two can defend themselves. A cord of three strands is not quickly broken.

—ECCLESIASTES 4:9–12 (NIV)

Iwant to be honest and talk about the struggles I've been having lately. How do you balance taking care of your house, family, husband, business, and yourself? To be honest, you don't. I got to the point where I was done. I couldn't keep going. I was questioning a lot of things.

When you decide to take leaps of faith that point others to a better way, you should expect to have troubles that pull you back. When you decide to use your story to bring others hope, you can expect troubles. I allowed every bit of trouble, animosity, negative thoughts, and doubts to flood my mind. I was tired of fighting. I was tired of the struggles. I was done. I needed a break.

I knew why everything was happening. I knew the source of it all. For a moment, for a day, for a week, for a month, he won. But what he didn't realize is that he didn't win the battle. I will be fighting harder than I've ever fought because I love the person I'm becoming. This year has been a roller coaster—from terrible to amazing. I am not perfect. I fail every day, but I get up each morning and try again. I can't do everything for everyone all the time. I need help, but I never tell anyone. I cry myself to sleep so no one sees the pain I'm really in or how hurt or broken I am.

When I look in the mirror I don't see beauty or the amazing person I am. I see a fat, ugly, useless person. I always tell myself I'm a horrible wife and mother. I don't think about my dad, because the pain hurts in the depths of my soul. See how easy it is to give up or believe you're nothing?

I struggle more than anyone could ever imagine. I usually look so happy, but I'm dying inside. I'm hurting. I feel alone in a crowded room. All I want is to feel loved and needed. I know I am loved so much more than I can imagine and that I am beautiful in my own way. I'm not a perfect wife or mother, but I try my best every day and give my family everything I have. It has taken a lifetime to get where I am today, with a whole lot of prayers and one day at a time.

I am not where I was, and I am not where I am going. Thank you for allowing me to open up and be honest. We don't have to struggle alone. We don't have to fight alone. We don't have to be perfect. It is *not* your job to do everything for everyone.

We can ask for help, and it won't make us any less than who we are. We are loved. We are valuable. We are enough. We are beautiful. We are not alone.

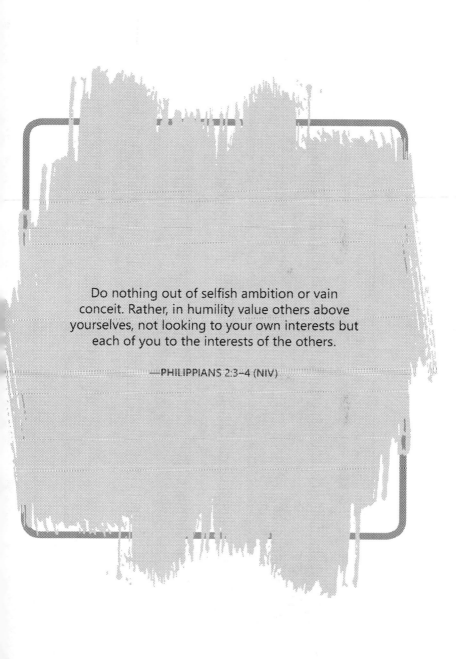

Do nothing out of selfish ambition or vain conceit. Rather, in humility value others above yourselves, not looking to your own interests but each of you to the interests of the others.

—PHILIPPIANS 2:3–4 (NIV)

S ometimes we have to fight for the ones we love. We have to believe even when they can't. Today my husband looked at me and said, "I think God favors him more than me."

In this moment my husband needed me. He didn't ask. He definitely didn't agree with my opinion, and he most certainly didn't know I was crying out to God for him too. I looked at him and really tried to figure out how in the world he could think he wasn't favored. How could he think he wasn't worthy?

He could only see one side of the story. He has no idea how incredible he truly is. His genuine love and compassion for others is extraordinary. His honesty is pure. He gives without ever asking for anything in return. I knew the moment when I hugged him for the first time that I'd spend the rest of my life with him. I knew I could tell my dad it was OK for him to die, because God had blessed me with such an incredible man who would fight for me when I couldn't fight for myself.

He would sit and hold me when I was crying on the floor, unable to get up from the pain from missing my dad. He would wipe the tears from my eyes and believe in me even when I don't believe in myself. He supports me even when I make it difficult. In that moment I refused to believe that James was brought back to life for a purpose far greater than what's happening right now. I refuse to believe he is favored and James is not. I refuse to believe that our current situation is the best. I refuse to believe we aren't enough or aren't lovable or that we don't have a greater purpose.

As a wife, a mom, and a friend, I have to believe in others for them. Sometimes the dark moments of life aren't ours, but belong to the ones we love and care for. In these moments it's OK to tell God how we feel. It's OK to tell Him it isn't fair. Sometimes the best way to help someone is to pray and believe for them.

God, You are the only One who can make the impossible way possible. You are the only One who can turn our can'ts into cans.

You are the only one who can break the chains and the walls that have us trapped.

God, we need you! We love you! We are waiting for you! Your will! Your way! Your dreams! Your blessings! When we can't think or speak, let these words ring out.

God, we need a miracle in our business, in our lives, in our marriage, in our kids. Use us to be a blessing to others. Use us to motivate, uplift, and lead others.

My hope and prayer are that you will fight for someone who can't fight for themselves and believe when others can't believe in themselves. You will love them when they can't love themselves. You will be there to help them when they can't help themselves.

God sees you! God hears you! Fight!

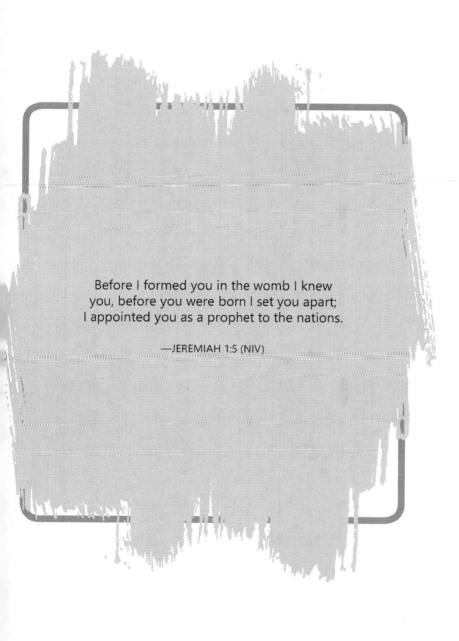

Before I formed you in the womb I knew
you, before you were born I set you apart;
I appointed you as a prophet to the nations.

—JEREMIAH 1:5 (NIV)

*A*t a point when my marriage was struggling at the same time as my son's health was suffering, it seemed like everything was wrong. I had to rely on God just to make it through the next hour. I'm not sure how I survived the mental attacks. I have often gone to God to ask him why this or that happened. *Why did my dad have to die?*

At that time I really had no one else to talk to *but* God. It was almost like God had somehow allowed all this to happen so that I'd be forced to press into God more than I ever had before. So God kind of became my best friend—one who didn't talk, but just listened.

I tend to think a lot. As I was thinking back over some of the lowest points of my life, I remembered one time that I'd never told anyone about. In a moment of desperation, I wanted my husband to know what was going on in my mind. I wanted him to understand times that I had struggled and why. We had been together for eighteen years and married for eleven. I hadn't told him in all that time.

It was while looking back over these moments when I slowly started to see the pieces of the puzzle fitting together. In that moment, I wondered what the purpose was of my dad dying. They say God will never call you home until you've completed the purpose you were created to do. I realized that maybe my dad's purpose in life had been to save mine. Had I not taken a moment to think about him and about how killing myself would destroy him, I may not have lived another night.

As the tears filled my eyes and my heart broke, this possibility slowly started to sink into my soul. What if my dad's purpose was really to save my life? I don't know if that is the case, but I do know that I am here in this moment writing this because of that moment on that night. Until I meet Jesus, I will never truly know, but what I do know is God called us to be the light of the world. He called us to be the hands and feet of Jesus and love others.

When you feel God leading you to share your story, take a leap of faith one day at a time. One day, you'll hopefully end up exactly where you're supposed to be, doing exactly what you're supposed to be doing. If my dad's purpose was to save my life, then there would have to be a greater purpose than the darkness I was lost in at the moment.

If I was made for more, then you are too! We have to keep fighting. We can't give up. We have to let go and trust God, no matter what.

God, thank You! Thank You for every precious soul who has taken the time to read this book. Lord, I pray that in moments when they are desperately needing You that You would bring peace and comfort to them.

God, when the darkness comes and they can't seem to get past it, send them rays of light that will shine brighter than the darkness they're lost in. I pray that as they seek You, they will find You. When they knock, I pray You will answer, according to Your will.

I pray that they spend time with You and seek Your plan and will for their lives. God, I pray You will be what they need in the moments they find themselves in.

I pray for Your love, grace, and mercy over their lives. Be with them. Guide them. I ask these things in Your precious name. Amen!

Never ever forget you are loved more than you will ever know by Someone who died for you.

Never be too afraid or ashamed to ask for help.
Reach out to a local church. There are a lot of great Christian radio stations that have counselors standing by to pray with you.

National Domestic Violence Hotline
(800) 799-7233

National Grad Crisis Line
(877) 472-3457

National Sexual Assault Hotline
(800) 656-4673

National Suicide Prevention Lifeline
(800) 273-8255

National Suicide Prevention Lifeline (Options for Deaf and Hard of Hearing)
For TTY Users: Use your preferred relay service or dial 711 then 1-800-273-8255

Substance Abuse and Mental Health Services Administration National Helpline
(800) 662-4357

Veterans Crisis Line
(800) 273-8255, PRESS 1

Text 838255
Childhelp National Child Abuse Hotline
(800) 422-4453

Crisis Text Line
Text HOME to 741741

Truths to cling to:
You are loved.
You are not alone.
You are worthy.
You are valued.
You are smart.
You are brave.
You are forgiven.
You are free.
Your story isn't over.
God loves you.
God values you.
God's ready to meet you where you are.
You are created for a purpose far greater than
the moment you find yourself in.

About The Author

Winter Hall is a devoted wife, mother, friend, and follower of Jesus. She is compassionate, caring, and loves wholeheartedly. Through her worst heartache, the death of her father in 2006, she found herself struggling. As her relationship with God grew, she realized that He was the only one who could sustain her. Her relationship with the Lord continues to grow.

Thank you to our company 2Fish Apparel LLC for making this dream possible.

Follow Our 2Fish Apparel Facebook Page @2fishapparelllc
Follow Our 2Fish Apparel Instagram Page @2fishapparel
Website: 2fishapparel.com
Email: 2fishapparel@gmail.com

Ways To Connect With Author

www.facebook.com/groups/madeformore145/
madeformore145@gmail.com

Printed in the United States
by Baker & Taylor Publisher Services